Mr. Mencken has also written

PREJUDICES—*six volumes*

SELECTED PREJUDICES · A BOOK OF BURLESQUES

THE AMERICAN LANGUAGE

A BOOK OF PREFACES · IN DEFENSE OF WOMEN

NOTES ON DEMOCRACY

TREATISE ON THE GODS

He has translated
THE ANTICHRIST
by F. W. Nietzsche

He has edited
MENCKENIANA: A SCHIMPFLEXIKON

He has written introductions to
VENTURES IN COMMON SENSE
by E. W. Howe

MAJOR CONFLICTS
by Stephen Crane

THE AMERICAN DEMOCRAT
by James Fenimore Cooper

These are Borzoi Books published by Alfred A. Knopf

MAKING
A PRESIDENT

MAKING
A PRESIDENT

A FOOTNOTE TO THE SAGA
OF DEMOCRACY

by

H. L. MENCKEN

New York *ALFRED · A · KNOPF* *Mcmxxxii*

Published September 1, 1932
Second Printing September, 1932

MANUFACTURED IN THE UNITED STATES
OF AMERICA

PREFACE

THE PIECES which follow, consisting mainly of my reports of the two national conventions of 1932 for the Baltimore *Evening Sun,* are not offered as history, but simply as its crude raw materials. There are not a few errors in them, of observation and of inference, and to one or two I have called attention in footnotes. Others were detected while the successive editions of the *Evening Sun* were spouting from the presses, and corrected either by bulletins from me, or by the alertness of the paper's editors and copyreaders. In one case I was saved from making a thumping bull by my colleague, Henry M. Hyde, a reporter whose immense professional skill is equaled only by his thoughtfulness for those who work with him. In another case a chance conversation late at night, while I was engaged upon a gin ricky in a state almost of nature, rescued me from a horrible misquotation from The Pilgrim's Progress, and so saved me from the mocking of my literary and theological friends. This last slip had been detected in the *Sunday Sun* office, but the hardworked brethren there had been unable to make out what I was really driving at. Some hurried telegraphing put them on the track, but the necessary emendations left my story short a paragraph that had adorned it.

I go into these details because the difficulties under which a newspaper man works seem to be but little understood by the great multitudes who read him. The news of the day does not spring into the world well formed and neatly labeled; it is, instead, a very ragged and imperfect thing in its native state, and it issues from the space-time continuum in most irregular spurts. The dispatch which appears here as No. XII is the final text of a series which began at 9 A. M. of June 28 and ran

until 3 P. M. During that time four different forms
of it got into as many editions of the *Evening Sun*
and some of those forms were made up of four
or five different sections, dispatched at different
times and even from different places. Part of the
thing was written at the *Sun's* quarters in the
Blackstone Hotel, part at the Western Union telegraph office in the Congress Hotel, and part at
one of the public writing-desks in the Congress
lobby, with a band playing nearby, and two or
three hundred people milling about. In the first
version to get into print, not four but five gory
bouts were forecast, but one of them—that over
the two-thirds rule—was abandoned by noon, and
after that there were only four. A little while later
the bout over the seating of the Louisiana Kingfish was settled, and there had to be another re-
casting. Meanwhile, the wet wets perfected their
minority Prohibition plank (to become the majority plank the next day), and it had to be substituted for the version sent earlier in the day. In
my souvenirs of the convention I find some carbons
of my successive corrections and substitutions.
They are almost unintelligible to me today, but
my colleagues of the *Evening Sun* copydesk

somehow fathomed them, and the blunders that remain in the dispatch as you will read it are all mine, not theirs.

The purely physical difficulties confronting a reporter told off to cover so vast and widely dispersed a thing as a national convention are extremely trying. What goes on in the actual hall is only part of it, and seldom the most important part. There are also four or five committees to think of, not to mention forty-eight State delegations, any one of which may throw a monkeywrench into the machinery at any moment. Each of the candidates also has his headquarters, and sometimes those headquarters are extensive labyrinths, with chambers that are secret as well as chambers where every comer is welcomed. Moreover, various other politicians of high potency are also on the scene, and every one of them, at very short notice or no notice at all, may begin to sweat important news. It would be manifestly impossible for any reporter, however sound his legs and wind, to cover all these rat-holes on his tours, so each has to depend upon exchanges with his friends. These exchanges are made freely, but they are often confusing and sometimes maddening, for

what Friend No. 1 says may be contradicted categorically by Friend No. 2, and both may be set
down as completely misinformed by Friends Nos.
3, 4, 5 and 6. Thus the conscientious newsman—
and in thirty-three years in journalism I have met
few who were not conscientious—must do a great
deal of gadding about on his own hook, and at the
end of a workday of sixteen hours or more, with
bands bombarding his ears, drunks jostling him
and elevators too jammed to carry him up and
down, he is likely to be pretty well used up.

I am conscious, on re-reading No. XVII, that a
tired air is apparent in it, but when I recall the
circumstances under which it was concocted I
marvel that it is not worse. The night before the
session it describes the convention had sat until
well after one o'clock, beating Prohibition to
death. I returned to the *Evening Sun* bureau in the
Blackstone Hotel at two or thereabout, and began
writing the dispatch which here appears as No.
XVI. But along about three o'clock I resolved to
postpone the rest until the morning, and so took a
bath and a drink and went to bed. I was up before
nine to resume my labors, and filed my last sheet
of copy at ten-thirty, in time to make the first edi-

tion of the *Evening Sun,* which closes at ten forty-five. (The difference in time between Baltimore and Chicago did not concern us of the *Sun,* for the fact that Chicago, with daylight time, was an hour behind Eastern Standard Time was offset by the fact that Baltimore did not follow daylight time.)

The convention met that evening at eight o'clock, and was in continuous session until nine the next morning. It took until four to make all the nomination speeches, and the first ballot was not finished until after five. I had had less than six hours sleep the night before, and no more the night before that, but I somehow managed to survive. During the early part of the night the heat in the hall was terrific, and all the brethren in the press-stand, like the delegates on the floor, were dripping with perspiration. As for me, my seersucker suit came to resemble a bathing-suit, and my neck-tie took on the appearance of having been fried. At three o'clock in the morning there was a violent thunder-storm and the temperature dropped. The cops, no longer beset by gate-crashers, for most of the spectators had gone home, opened wide the huge doors of the hall, and a cool breeze swept through. It made me sleepy and I went out to the parking-space next to the hall to shake myself awake. There I met Walter Lippmann, and we sat down on the step of an automobile to discuss the sorrows of the Republic. When I got back to the stand Will Rogers was in my seat, and we had a jawing match for half an hour. The balloting had begun by then, and it was to drag on for nearly five hours. At seven o'clock I went out for breakfast. It consisted of a roast beef sandwich and a glass of beer.

When I got back there was a notice from the *Evening Sun* office that its first edition for the day was to be pushed up from ten forty-five to nine o'clock, and I was ordered to get busy for it. I had left my typewriter at the hotel, which was two or three miles away, so I had to fall on the job with a lead-pencil. It was hard work, for I have been doing all my writing on the machine since boyhood, but the prodding of Paul Patterson kept me moving, and I was well into the story before the session adjourned. Then I returned to the Blackstone and finished it. I got to bed at 11.30 A. M. At 5.15 I was routed out by a telephone call, and did not get back to bed. The session that night was mercifully short. It began at nine o'clock and was over before eleven. But before I turned in I had to write and file the better part of No. XVIII. A tough two days!

No. VI also caught me without my typewriter. I was drowsing in the stand when former Senator France popped up, and began to do his extraordinary stuff. France was a minor character in the convention drama, but he was a Marylander and thus of special interest to the *Evening Sun* and its customers. Moreover, it was then late in the afternoon, and there was no time to lose. So I had to leap for the hoosegow where the cops had him caged, and find out what his uproar was about. In a few minutes I was back in the stand and at work, with Paul Patterson acting as my city editor. His elbow kept me diligent, and No. VI went to Baltimore in eleven pieces. The first two or three were set up, printed and on the street before the last one left the press-stand. It would not be Christian to demand literary graces in compositions so confected. If they present the facts coherently they have gone far enough. But even more important is speed. And speed with a lead-pencil, with bands playing and twenty thousand people howling, saps the soul.

PREFACE

Perhaps, having proceeded so far with my somewhat irrelevant confidences, I may as well add a few lines about the arrangements that a big newspaper makes for covering a national convention. The *Sunpaper*, which has both morning and evening editions, took six men to Chicago—Paul Patterson, J. Fred. Essary, Frank R. Kent, James Bone, Henry M. Hyde and me. Patterson is president of the company publishing the paper, and a reporter and editor of long experience: he acted as editor in the field, and apportioned the work of the rest of us. Essary is the chief of the *Sun's* Washington bureau, and Kent is its political expert. Bone is London editor of the Manchester *Guardian*, with which the *Sun* has a news exchange arrangement: he did both a daily cable for his own paper and a daily article for the *Sun*. Hyde has spent most of his time of late covering Senatorial investigations in Washington for the *Evening Sun*. In Chicago we were joined by W. A. S. Douglas, the *Sun's* Chicago correspondent, and for the Democratic convention by John W. Owens, editor of the *Sun* and once a member of its Washington staff.

The aim of this outfit was not so much to cover

the news of the two conventions as to interpret it. The routine of fact was handled by the press associations, and in addition the *Sun* had access to all the reports of the Chicago *Tribune*. For the morning edition Essary wrote the daily lead—and sometimes he had to write it five or six times!—, Kent wrote the political article that he contributes to the *Sun* every day (naturally, it was much expanded), Douglas wrote whatever interested him (mainly stuff about the more picturesque characters in the comedy), and Bone set down his impressions as a visitor from foreign parts. For the *Evening Sun* Hyde undertook the herculean task of writing a daily story from the stand, and I did whatever I was put to. Hyde's job was probably the hardest of all, for he had to produce a connected and coherent account of events while they were actually happening, and to get it in at the speed demanded by an evening newspaper with many editions. There were days when he sat in his place for four or five hours on end, with a telegraph boy at his elbow, and one day he wrote fully four columns.

We had a leased wire running from the hotel, and another running from an office under the press-stand. But a good deal of our stuff, written neither at the hotel nor at the hall, went over the ordinary commercial wires. How many words we filed altogether I don't know, but there was at least one day when the total was about twenty thousand. Douglas found an excellent operator in Chicago, and I set down his name with gratitude, for he sent my own copy quickly and accurately. He was a Mr. Wexler, a Russian born in England, and he had as his aide another good operator, Miss Knutson. To run copy for us and do other such jobs we had at different times, three young men, one of them Patterson's son McLean. These youngsters had plenty to do. I marvel indeed that they got to the end of the Democratic convention without wearing down their legs to the knees. So much for the record. I set it down mainly for newspaper men, who are always interested in how their colleagues work.

My failures as a prophet are here embalmed shamelessly. I was sorely tempted to expunge some of them, but managed to refrain. My consolation must lie in the fact that all of the other journalists who adorned the scene fell into the same snares, and that most of the politicians—

PREFACE

consider, for example, Al Smith!—did a great deal worse.

My indebtedness to the *Evening Sun* for permission to reprint my contributions to it is manifest. It is not new, for all of my "Prejudices" books were made up in considerable part of such contributions.

H. L. M.

CONTENTS

CONTENTS

MAKING
A PRESIDENT

—I—

EXPLANATORY AND HISTORICAL

[From the American Mercury, June, 1932]

———————————

A WEEK or so after these lines are flung to the world two thousand men and women will gather in Chicago to nominate a successor to Lord Hoover. Two or three weeks later another couple of thousand will gather in the same place to do the same thing. The former will constitute the delegates and alternates to the Republican National Convention; the latter will have the same character at the convention of the Democrats. It will take the Republican brothers and sisters no longer than a day to perform their work, for Lord Hoover himself will be the only serious candidate before them; nevertheless, they will stretch out the business to four days at least, and maybe five, and all the while they will sit uncomfortably on hard kitchen chairs by day, and sweat and pant through packed hotel lobbies at night.

All of this will be done at their own expense. They will buy their own tickets to Chicago and their own tickets home, and they will pay for their own board and lodging. For it is considered a high honor, by American standards of value, to be elected a delegate or alternate to a Republican national convention, and persons who have enjoyed it always mention it when they are asked (as, for example, by the editor of "Who's Who in America") what they have achieved in the world. Moreover, something tangible commonly goes with the glory of it, for when election day is over a large proportion of the delegates and alternates find themselves settled in very pleasant Federal jobs, ranging from that of Secretary of State to that of United States marshal for the northern district of Louisiana. In normal times, indeed, the majority of them are already in lucrative office when they go to the convention, so their minds are suffused, as they squirm upon the hot, hard chairs or fall over the spittoons in the hotel lobbies, by very agreeable reflections.

The Democrats, impaled upon the same chairs, enjoy no such consolation. It is their common doom to go home from their convention in a low and even tortured frame of mind, with their pocket-books empty, their larynxes frayed, the seats of their pantaloons worn shiny, and a candidate on their hands whose chances of election are a good deal worse than bad. But they sit and suffer just as faithfully as the Republicans, and in fact even more faithfully, for it is rare for their convention to be finished in a week, and sometimes it lasts for three weeks. At New York, in 1924, many of them ran so short of money, what with the notorious seductions and extortions of the town, that they had to telegraph home for more, and in some of the Southern constituencies public subscriptions for their relief were taken up, and the Methodist and Baptist pastors prayed desperately that they might be sustained long enough to scotch the Roman Harlot. Yahweh granted that prayer, but added a characteristic jocosity, in His usual bad taste. That is, He bewitched them into nominating the Hon. John W. Davis, of Wall Street, W. Va., and at the ensuing plebiscite John got a beating that was astonishing, even for a Democrat.

This year there will be more hope, but probably not much. As I write only one aspirant, the Hon. Franklin D. Roosevelt, LL.D., appears to be really formidable, and if Democrats were Republicans he would be nominated quickly and quietly, and the whole show would be over by Friday morning of convention week. But the Democrats never do things in any such marshmallow way. They are not really a party, but two parties, and between the two there is a flaming and implacable antagonism. Thus one looks confidently for a ruction in the grand manner when they gather at Chicago, following the love-feast of the Republicans. The Southern drys and the Northern wets, both full of the same Capone booze, will fall upon one another with loud challenges and imprecations, and after a week or so of dog-and-cat fighting the proceedings will end with all hands worn out and full of despair. Of the platform only one thing may be predicted: that it will please nobody. And of the candidate only one thing also: that he will be suspected by all.

On August 26, 1920, when the Nineteenth

Amendment was proclaimed, I offered the prediction that it would cause alcoholism to be displaced, as the chief weakness of American politicians, by adultery. But this prophecy was rather too romantic: my excuse for it is that I had yet to see any considerable number of lady politicians. They are, taking one with another, far more dissuasive than the Seventh Commandment, and so the old smell of booze continues to hang over every national convention. At the last Republican affair, at Kansas City, there was enough of the stuff to float the Atlantic Fleet, and some of the most distinguished statesmen in attendance were corned all the time. One of them, a passionate and eminent dry, wolfed a whole quart of Missouri Scotch every evening, and then had to be given another quart, wrapped up in the Kansas City *Star*, to get rid of him. The Law Enforcement plank in the platform was adopted to a veritable simoon of hiccups, and not a few delegates and alternates had to be taken to spas when the Apostle of the Noble Experiment was finally nominated.

The Democrats at Houston had a dryer time of it, but only because the town's booticians failed them. One of the local philanthropists, eager to succor them, took a parlor in a hotel, fitted it up as a bar, put in twenty or thirty barrels of beer out of his private stock, and invited the visitors to come in and help themselves, but not many responded, for what Democrats crave is hard liquor, and the harder it is the better they like it. Beer is poison to a Southern dry, and so is wine. His system demands corn whiskey fresh from the still, and in Houston there was not enough of it to go round. So the convention broke up in even worse humor than usual, and most of the Southerners, in the November following, voted for Hoover. This year the National Committee had sense enough not to choose Houston again, or any other such place. Instead it selected Chicago, where the booze supply is endless, and even Southern drys can be accommodated.

The Republicans commonly carry their liquor better than the Democrats, just as they commonly wear their clothes better. One seldom sees one of them actively sick in the convention hall, or dead drunk in a hotel lobby. Even the colored brethren among them are considerably more refined than the white Democrats from the Christian Endeavor Belt. These colored brethren, by the time they reach the convention hall, are nearly all bought and paid for, and so there is nothing for them to do save to vote as their purchasers order. They seldom make speeches, and never engage in fights. If one of them pulled a razor at a Republican national convention the indecorum would be sufficient to ruin him. But the white Democrats are often very bellicose, and it is nothing unusual for them to slug one another on the floor. At Houston (or was it New York?) there was a dreadful fight among the delegates from one of the great Christian States of the South. It came after the candidate was nominated, and while the State standards were being paraded about the floor. The standard of this State was seized by a delegate who was suspected of being an agnostic, and two of his Baptist colleagues protested against the sacrilege and undertook to maul him. It took a whole squad of police to restore order.

The delegates, as I have hinted, have to submit to a considerable physical discomfort. The chairs that they occupy are not only hard, but also very narrow, and they are so placed that there is little knee-room. Thus a delegate who draws a seat near the middle of the row is stuck there for hours. If he struggles out to send a telegram to his pastor, or for any other natural purpose, he is hustled and sworn at by those he incommodes, and on returning to the hall he is very apt to be held up by a cop, and maybe roughed before he is identified. Not a few delegates, getting tight, lose their badges on the evening of the first day, and remain in the uncomfortable position of alien enemies until the appropriate officials can be induced to do something about it. At the New York convention, in 1924, one of the lady delegates, a woman of commanding presence, found that the seat given to her was two or three feet too narrow, so she had a large armchair brought into the hall, and plumped it in the main aisle. She was thus comfortable enough, but when the parading began many a delegate fell over her façade and bawled her out in a hearty and chivalrous manner.

Not many women politicians are as fat as that one, but in general they run to a considerable heft and beam. My somewhat indelicate prediction of August 26, 1920, hitherto mentioned, was based on the theory that, with the vote in their hands, many cuties would horn into politics, and that as a result the more susceptible male politicians, engaged at a national convention with their wives far away, would forget themselves. But nothing of the sort seems to have happened: the lady delegates and alternates are commonly too mature in years and too robust in figure to inspire romance. Moreover, conventions are always held in hot weather, and so they perspire fearfully, and that fact also discourages amour. When a fair delegate of any actual pulchritude shows up she makes a sensation, and is so busy being photographed for the rotogravures and news-reels that she is seldom seen on the convention floor. The drys hoped that the presence of women would hold down the traditional boozing, but that hope has not been realized. The brethren still hasten to get themselves outside whatever they can find. The only difference is that the Republicans, having loaded up, sleep it off quietly, whereas the Democrats whoop and yell.

I have been going to national conventions, off and on, since 1900, and note some sad changes. One is the virtual disappearance of oratory. I recall very vividly the late William Jennings Bryan's farewell speech at St. Louis in 1904, after Alton B. Parker, a Wall Street werewolf, had been nominated. It was a truly superb effort, and veterans of 1896 agreed that it was clearly better than the Cross of Gold speech. Give me a *Lis'l of Helles,* to recall Tony Faust's, and I can hear its peroration yet: "You may say that I have not run a good race, you may say that I have not fought a good fight, *but no man shall say that I have not kept the faith!*" The ensuing uproar almost put the kibosh upon poor Parker: it took some sharp work by the leaders to prevent the delegates stampeding to Bryan. He had practised the speech for days, and delivered it in a husky, sepulchral voice, on the theory that he was ill. Whether he was really ill or not I don't know, but if he was, then he had certainly recovered completely by the next morning.

Such gaudy harangues will never be heard again, for the loud-speaker now reduces all voices to one metallic roar. Even the lady politicians, when they are allowed to second a motion and show off their millinery, sound like auctioneers. The crowd in the gallery quickly tires of such noise, and is not above booing it. At the Coolidge convention in Cleveland, in 1924, a bald-headed orator from somewhere in the South got on his hind legs and proceeded to loose some old-time rhetoric. The gallery began to jeer him at once, and presently even the delegates joined in. The Southern brother kept at it manfully—a lot of scarlet stuff comparing Coolidge to the rising sun, the precession of the equinoxes, the aurora borealis, and so on—but in the end the platform catchpolls had to close in on him. For his sufferings on this painful occasion he was rewarded with a Federal judgeship, and is now one of the great ornaments of American jurisprudence, with a bishop's power to bind and loose. To mention his name might get me ten years at Leavenworth or the Dry Tortugas.

Inasmuch as every delegate has to pay his own expenses only patriots who are relatively well heeled can aspire to the office. The costs of the convention itself are commonly met by blackmailing the hotel-keepers of the convention town, and they always try to get their money back by raising their rates, often to preposterous levels. I have myself paid as much as $20 a night for a room that, in ordinary times, surely did not fetch more than $4. In the old days the local hack-drivers also took large bites at the visitors, but of late, with standardized taxicabs everywhere, they are no longer rooked in transit between their hotels and the hall, even when in their cups. Most of the delegates make a holiday of their trip, and try to compensate themselves for the hard chairs they have to sit on all day by cutting up at night. Those from small towns swarm to the burlesque theatres, night clubs, bawdy-houses and other such free-and-easies of the convention city: they see and hear enough marvels in a week to talk about for the rest of their lives. The more sophisticated confine themselves to quiet lushing. The so-called leaders, if there is no caucus in progress, play poker in their headquarters, or expose themselves to the public veneration in the hotel lobbies. An eminent United States Senator, once a serious contender for the Presidency, used to have his secretary circulate in the crowd, to point him out and whisper his great deeds. Others have themselves paged. Now and then a wag hires a bellboy to page Abraham Lincoln or Pontius Pilate.

As I have said, the fund to pay for a convention—it costs about $150,000—is usually raised by sweating the hotel-keepers of the convention city, with some assistance from the bootleggers and other purveyors of entertainment, but now and then the town boosters take charge, and there is a formal drive. This drive is promoted on the theory that a convention brings a great deal of money to a city, and advertises it widely. But what really happens, nine times out of ten, is that the city gets a black eye. Either the hotels gouge the visitors too ferociously, or the booze supply is insufficient, or the weather is too hot, or there is something else to complain of. The delegates and alternates go home complaining loudly, and so do the newspaper reporters, who commonly outnumber them, and the result is that the city suffers damage from which it is years recovering.

Consider, for example, the case of Cleveland, which entertained the Coolidge convention in 1924. The delegates and alternates went there expecting the town to be wide open, for wasn't Coolidge already President, and weren't Prohibition agents men of enlightened self-interest? But Cal forgot or refused to give the word, and in consequence a huge swarm of agents descended upon the town, and it was as dry as the Sahara. So dry was it, in fact, that even the local newspaper men had nothing to drink: a revolting and almost incredible fact, but still a fact. I well remember saving the life of a distinguished Middle Western statesman, a conscientious dry. He was seized with a severe bellyache, caused by the Lake Erie water, and I found him on the street almost doubled up. I called a policeman, but the cop told me in tears, and I believe truthfully, that he simply didn't know where a drink was to be had. Fortunately, I recalled the fact that Ring Lardner was in a nearby hotel, writing a news report of next day's session, and to him I took the patient. Lardner had him well in twenty seconds.

This astounding dryness did more harm to Cleveland than an earthquake or a pestilence. It sent 1000 delegates, 1000 alternates and 1000 newspaper reporters home with horrible stories of the rigors of life in the town. Those stories still circulate, and even gain in wonder as the years pass.[1] Certainly they must keep thousands of visitors away, and implant dubieties in the hearts of many potential investors. In the same manner Baltimore still suffers from the fact that it

[1] After these paragraphs were printed in the *American Mercury* various Cleveland boosters came forward with denials that the town was actually dry in 1924. But I have 3000 witnesses who know and are willing to swear that they lie.

entertained the Wilson convention in 1912. The weather at the time was excessively hot, and the hall was remote from the principal hotels. As a result, all the persons in attendance at the convention suffered cruelly and made loud lamentation, and to this day, whenever I meet one of them, he recalls his agonies and damns the town. The common belief that Baltimore is so hot in Summer that only ship's firemen and colored clergymen can stand it originated during that convention. It will take half a century to live it down.

The only American city that has ever got any ponderable profit out of entertaining a national convention is San Francisco. It has, in June, very mild and caressing weather, and its visionaries long ago erected a comfortable meeting hall. When, in 1920, the Democrats assembled in that hall to nominate a successor to the immortal Woodrow, they wallowed in unaccustomed luxury. Instead of the usual filthy hot-dog stands in the lobby there was a clean lunchroom served by sweeties in lovely uniforms. Instead of ward heelers armed with clubs to police the aisles there were more sweeties, each with a demure white

wand. Instead of decorations fit for a street car-
nival, there were draperies in various shades of
green, with a single American flag. And instead
of bad liquor at high prices there was an ample
supply of sound Bourbon, absolutely free of
charge.

Who supplied this Bourbon I don't know.
There were allegations later on that it had been
laid in by the city of San Francisco in person,
and charged to the town smallpox hospital. Some
of the town wowsers, in fact, made an uproar
about it, and there were denunciations of the
mayor, the Hon. James Rolph, Jr. The more enlightened people of the city answered by reëlect-
ing him almost unanimously, and he remained
gloriously in office until a year or so ago, when
he became Governor and Captain-General of
California. As for the delegates and alternates
to the convention, they drank the Bourbon with
loud hosannahs. At the end of the first week,
though their business was completed, they refused to go home, but adjourned over to Monday.
Sunday morning saw hundreds of them start out
in taxicabs to see the sights, each armed with a
flagon of the Bourbon. Some of these taxicabs

were recovered later on at points as far distant as San Diego and Seattle.

This was the most pleasant national convention ever held in America, and those who were in attendance have been fanatics for San Francisco ever since. Every four years, when the Democratic National Committee meets to select the convention city, there are demands that San Francisco be chosen again. The Republican National Committee is also beset by such demands, for the Republican politicians have all heard about the grand time their Democratic colleagues had there in 1920, and sweat under the humiliating fact that they themselves, since the fatal January 16 of that year, have never had a really satisfying convention. But the master-minds of both great parties, though they always say nice things about San Francisco, are actually somewhat suspicious of it, for they fear that the next convention held there may be reduced to actual chaos. It is very hard to hold the delegates and alternates to their jobs when such excellent liquor is on tap.

New York got only ill fame out of the Democratic convention of 1924, holden in Madison

Square Garden, now no more. If it had been a Republican convention it might have passed off pleasantly enough, for the Republican delegates, in the main, are city-broke, but the Democrats from the cotton country were greatly upset by what they saw of life in the American Gomorrah. In particular, they were scared by the New York cops and by the swarms of Romish priests who appeared in the galleries and on the platform. All of them had been taught by their pastors that priests carried stilettos, and they believed it. Moreover, they believed that when the priests began to hack and slay, the local police, all of them customers of Rome, would join in the massacre with artillery.

This may sound like spoofing, but it is a sober fact. One day, while a furious wrangle was in progress on the floor, I went to a small room under the stand, reserved for the staff of the Baltimore *Sunpapers*, and proceeded to compose an account of it. In a few minutes the door opened and an eminent Southern statesman popped in. Closing and bolting the door, he whispered: "They are about to kill us!"

"Who?" I asked.

"The Tammany police!"

"Nonsense!"

"I tell you it is a fact! I saw one of them sneaking up on me on the floor! They are about to cut loose!"

Inasmuch as this statesman was one of the few really dry drys that I have ever met or heard of, it was impossible for me to calm him in the usual manner, so I had to find a couple of Tammany men to reassure him. They took him to a nearby hotel, gave him a Bible to read, and promised to stand guard at his door.

It was at this convention that the Al Smith men paved the way for Al's defeat four years later. They filled the galleries with Tammany hoodlums armed with fire-engine sirens, and howled down every anti-Smith man who ventured to speak. Worse, they packed the hall with the aforesaid priests, and so kept the Ku Kluxers from the Bible country in constant terror. I am, in general, partial to the rev. clergy, but I must confess that many of these New York brethren, with their sacerdotal corporations and beetling brows, looked like pretty tough guys. The police, if anything, were even worse. Thus the Southerners went home in great agitation of mind, and had bad dreams for months. And when the chance came four years later they flocked to the polls to vote for Lord Hoover. If the vote in the South had been counted honestly in 1928 he would have carried every Southern State, and some of them almost unanimously.

I set down these random recollections and observations in the hope that they will throw some light upon the manner in which Presidents of the Republic are chosen, and by whom. The common belief seems to be that they are heaved into the White House by a spontaneous popular demand, and that if anyone has any hand in shaping that demand it is not the professional politicians, but the hell-hounds of Wall Street. But this is a romantic and inaccurate view of what happens. The candidate who really gets the nomination is that candidate who has the most delegates, and the way he gets them is not by making speeches or by seeing J. Pierpont Morgan, but by dealing confidentially with the politicians in the various States. In 1920 Lord Hoover was certainly a thousand times as notorious and popular as the Hon. Warren Gamaliel Harding, and yet

Hoover, trying desperately for the nomination, lost it, and it went to Harding.

That sad experience taught him something: in fact, it converted him into a very realistic politician. During the eight years following he had his agents at work from end to end of the country, seeing the local politicians and bringing them in line. This business cost a great deal of money, but Hoover was rich and could afford it. When the Kansas City convention met in 1928 he had so many delegates in his corral that his nomination was a walk-over. All of the Southern blackamoors bore his brand, and so did most of the survivors of the Ohio Gang and other such amenable sodalities. His operating staff on the floor consisted of some of the most adept manipulators in America. In fact, he had almost a monopoly of the real technicians, and so he won hands down, to the inspiring strains of "America" *geb.* "God Save the King!"

It is to be noted that Wall Street was firmly against Hoover, and hoped until the last moment to beat him. Old Andy Mellon, its ambassador on the floor, held out gallantly until Bill Vare of Pennsylvania, who had been prudently seen and taken in advance, pulled his legs from under him, and made an obscene spectacle of him. Many a statesman of national fame, unaware or incredulous of the skill of Hoover's agents, kept on howling against him up to the moment of his nomination. One such was old Charlie Curtis, the Kansas comic character, who is half Indian and half windmill. Charlie ran against Hoover with great energy, and let fly some very embarrassing truths about him. But when the Hoover managers, having collared the nomination for their employer, threw Charlie the Vice-Presidency as a solatium, he shut up instantly, and a few days later he was hymning his late bugaboo as the greatest statesman since Pericles.

It always amuses me to hear Hoover spoken of as a poor politician. He is actually one of the most skillful in all this broad Republic, and if he did not begin to pursue the art seriously until after 1920 then his extraordinary virtuosity to-day is only a proof of his great natural talent. Few men with an itch for office have ever learned the tricks so quickly, or so well. History has already amassed enough evidence to show that he was never an engineer of any genuine dignity, and I am convinced that even the school-books of the future will put him down as a sad flop as President. But as politician pure and simple he has been a great success. He got the nomination in 1928 by playing politics in the most orthodox and shameless manner, he was elected by stooping to devices that even most professional politicians would balk at, and he will be renominated in a few weeks with the aid of one of the most efficient and unconscionable political machines ever heard of.

His probable opponent, Dr. Roosevelt, is another adept. The manner in which he has isolated, hamstrung and made a thumping fool of Al Smith must delight every connoisseur of political manipulation. At a time when Governor Ritchie, Dr. Baker, Alfalfa Bill Murray and the other Democratic candidates were filling the ether with learned discourses on the issues of the hour, Roosevelt had his agents out in the highways and byways, rounding up delegates. He did not bother to say much himself, and in particular he avoided saying anything that could conceivably offend anyone. On Prohibition, for example, he was completely silent for a whole year. But he was

busy all the while with the professional politicians, and when the time came to count up the
votes it turned out that he had more of them than
all the other candidates put together. When he
spoke, it was always shrewdly and to good effect.
His onslaught upon Rabbi Stephen S. Wise and
the Rev. John Haynes Holmes was well timed
and devastating. It not only reassured Tammany;
it also delighted millions of Democrats in the
Bible Belt, where religion is a perennial nui-
sance, and every sufferer from it likes to see the
clergy walloped.

A national convention is so constituted that
the candidate who avoids all dangerous talk and
confines himself quietly to rounding up delegates
has an enormous advantage. Nine-tenths of these
delegates are professional politicians; hence
they are but little interested in so-called issues;
the one thing that really fetches them is the promise of jobs. Some of them come from constituencies which have no votes—the Canal Zone, Porto
Rico, the Philippines, and so on. The rest, though
they represent enfranchised States, are apportioned in an irrational and even insane manner.
Thus such incurably Democratic States as Mis-

sissippi and South Carolina have virtually as many votes in the Republican convention as they have in the Democratic convention, and the same is true in the other direction of such rock-ribbed Republican States as Vermont and Iowa. The result is that a convention is made up in large part of delegates who represent, not voters, but simply politicians. The wise candidates goes out after these politicians very early, and knows how to persuade them. This was done by Lord Hoover before 1928, and by Dr. Roosevelt beginning a year ago.

One may ask why, if this be true, old Charlie Curtis did not devote more of his time and steam to rounding up delegates before the 1928 convention. There are three answers. The first is that he actually tried to do so, got a few in the Middle West, and allowed certain humorous politicians to fool him into thinking that he would get more. The second is that he lacked Lord Hoover's bar'l, could not find an angel to finance him, and hence had to keep out of the Southern States, where only cash money counts. The third is that Charlie, like most other politicians who have been quartered in Washington for a long while, greatly overestimated the general demand for him. Flattered by newspaper reporters, who found him an easy source of news, he concluded that he was a popular hero, and that the politicians would have to come to him. But this was an error. They never do. If the Cid without money were running against Judas Iscariot with $2,000,-000, they would all be in favor of Judas.

If I had a son I should take him to both national conventions this year and let him see how his country is governed, and by what sort of men and women. All of the leading statesmen, save a few austere spirits at the top of the heap, appear in person. Practically every member of the United States Senate is in attendance at either one convention or the other, and most of the members of the House are delegates.[2] It is instructive to observe these great men at the solemn business of selecting a First Chief for the greatest free Republic ever seen on earth. One hears, in their speeches, such imbecilities as even a Methodist conference could not match. One sees

[2] This, of course, was not true at Chicago, for Congress remained in session until both conventions were over. Nevertheless, a great many Congressmen sneaked away for each show, and at the Democratic convention at least fifteen Senators were on hand.

them at close range, sweating, belching, munching peanuts, chasing fleas. They parade idiotically, carrying dingy flags and macerating one another's corns. They crowd the aisles, swapping gossip, most of it untrue. They devour hot dogs. They rush out to the speakeasies.[3] They rush back to yell, fume and vote.

The average delegate never knows what is going on. The hall is in dreadful confusion, and the speeches from the platform are mainly irrelevant and unintelligible. The real business of a national convention is done down under the stage, in dark and smelly rooms, or in hotel suites miles away. Presently a State boss fights his way out to his delegation on the floor, and tells his slaves what is to be voted on, and how they are to vote. Many of them, on account of the din, cannot hear him. They cup their hands to their ears and say "Hey?" When he departs they demand "What

[3] At Chicago there was a very efficient speakeasy directly opposite the hall. Delegates and alternates were admitted on their badges, and so were newspaper reporters. Unfortunately, one of the Hearst reporters committed the incredible *faux pas* of writing a story about it, giving its name and location, and within an hour after that story was printed Prohibition agents raided the place. The local police thereupon guided the delegates to other speakeasies, but none was so convenient as the one closed.

did he say?" Sometimes, worn out by the hard benches and the deafening uproar, a whole delegation goes on a steamboat excursion, gets drunk, or decides to sleep all day. Then there is a great pother until the missing are rounded up.

During the first day or two the so-called platform committee holds long hearings in a smaller hall, sometimes far distant. All sorts of world-savers appear before it and demand that their gospels be inserted into the platform in toto— reformers of the calendar, advocates of the League of Nations, Red baiters of a hundred different factions, bogus war veterans demanding ever larger and larger bonuses, critics of Marine rule in Haiti and Nicaragua, Single Taxers, friends of the Porto Ricans and Filipinos, free trade fanatics, and so on. The committee hears these brethren patiently, but without promising anything. The platform was written weeks before the convention assembled, and has been passed as harmless by all the great minds of the party. If there is a fight over it on the floor, these great minds always win.[4] In the old days a gang of

[4] I should have said usually, not always. At the Democratic convention at Chicago they were beaten on Prohibition, and even at the Republican convention they had to yield a good

wild and shaggy Irish appeared at every convention to demand justice for Ireland, at the cost,
if necessary, of immediate war with England,
but of late they have been missed. I marvel that
the Communists do not slip into the vacant place.

To cover this colossal clown show at least 1000
newspaper men and women come to the convention town. They occupy seats adjoining the platform, and have a good view of the proceedings.
They are forbidden by traditional etiquette to
applaud or hiss a speaker, but they do a great
deal of quiet laughing, and altogether, despite
the rush of their work, have a much better time
of it than the delegates and alternates. At critical
moments many delegates rush up to ask them
what is going on; it is commonly impossible to
make out from the floor. Mingled with these professional journalists are eminent public figures
who have been employed by newspaper chains
to write their impressions of the spectacle—for
example, Will Rogers and Gene Tunney. At
times when he was not a candidate the late William Jennings Bryan used to be among them. He

deal to the roaring wets. But Prohibition is breaking all the
normal rules of American politics. On other questions the
Master-Minds almost invariably win.

always predicted that the Democratic party was about to be delivered from Wall Street, and that it would then sweep the country.

But I must shut down, for many able contributors to the present issue of the *American Mercury* are waiting to be heard. This modest note upon a great democratic phenomenon, in fact, has already run to an inordinate length, and I apologize to the nobility and gentry for being so garrulous. My excuse must be that the subject interests me very much. It is always instructive to examine into the way the work of the world is done, and especially that part of its work which is everybody's business. The selection of a President is obviously the concern of every American. Well, two things about it deserve to be noted. One is that it is done by professional politicians, and by professional politicians exclusively, and that at least nine-tenths of them can be bought, if not with downright money, then at all events with jobs. The other is that it is a purely extralegal proceeding—that there is no mention of the process in the Constitution, and that even the laws take little notice of it.

This last fact is very curious. We live in the

most law-ridden country on earth, and yet we manage to select our candidates for its highest office in a wholly informal manner, without the slightest aid from courts and policemen. A national convention is free to change its rules as it pleases. It may expel a delegate at will, and seat another. It may increase or diminish the representation of a State. It may seat delegates, if it chooses, from Turkestan or the moon. To be sure, certain States have passed laws regulating the election of delegates, but the number to be elected is still determined by agencies quite outside those States.

The system has been in operation for nearly a century, and on the whole it has worked pretty well. There have been no great scandals about it. There is nowhere any active desire to bring it under the protection of statutes. No one proposes seriously that it be abandoned. There is even no general talk about reforming it. What all this proves, it seems to me, is that government is far less necessary than many people think. When men are really in earnest they can get on very well without it. If national conventions were legalized, then the only effect would be to bring

the politicians who now run them under the heel
of even worse politicians.

—II—

THE REPUBLICANS
ASSEMBLE

[From the Baltimore Evening Sun, June 13, 1932]

Chicago, June 13

THE WETS, on this last day before the second
Hoover convention, are doing all of the talking,
and most of it is plentifully loud. It would be
more accurate, in fact, to describe it as a roaring.
Never in this life have I been witness to a more
pervasive confidence, a showier or more bellicose cockiness. The contrast with four years ago
is really amazing. At Kansas City all of the salient statesmen of the party talked dry, even when
they guzzled wet, but now many of them are
leaping on the beer-wagon with shrill jubilations,
and every hour or so a new convert is announced.

MAKING A PRESIDENT

If platforms were settled in hotel lobbies there would be nothing left to do save play "The Star-Spangled Banner" and open the saloons.

Unfortunately, the thing is not so simple, and my guess is that there will be a considerable amelioration of this wet ecstasy before the ceremonies in the stadium are concluded. Lord Hoover, as I write, is yet to be heard from, and no one believes seriously that if, when and as he speaks he will say anything properly describable as a repudiation of Prohibition. The most anyone hopes from him is a grudging and equivocal approval of resubmission, and the more intelligent wets are well aware that resubmission will leave them with their heaviest fight still ahead of them. What they all yearn and pant for is outright repeal, but outright repeal is surely not going into the Republican platform.

Thus the professional drys, despite the roaring of the wets, sit tight, and there is no real reason why they should be alarmed. Two massive facts stand in their favor. One is that they still have their collar around the neck of Lord Hoover, and that he dreads them far too much to throw it off at this stage of what may be a close and nasty fight. The other is that the wet leadership is still amateurish and ineffective, and is thus likely to round up far more whoops than actual votes. So the drys stick to their guns and are confident, too, though they make much less noise than the wets.

The chief hope of the wets lies in a wild and anarchistic revolt on the floor, with the delegates running amuck. To further it they have brought up some guns of high caliber, including the indefatigable President Nicholas Murray Butler of Columbia. He issued a deafening salvo when he got in yesterday and he has been violently in action ever since. Unfortunately, history teaches us that it is not the habit of Republican national conventions to pay much heed to such men as Dr. Butler, despite their shining wisdom. The majority of delegates are always found, when the roll is called, to be on the side of whoever has the giving out of jobs, and that business is now firmly in the hands of the great Australian engineer.

Many of the colored delegates from the South, at this minute, are suffering sadly at his hands. His agents are trying to throw them out and seat lily whites in their places. Nevertheless, these patriotic blackamoors, like their white colleagues, incline to be in favor of any great moral cause that Mr. Hoover is in favor of, and if the committee on credentials seats them, which seems likely, they will follow his inspired leadership up the old hills of Zion.

Hoover, as everyone knows, has his deficiencies as a leader, but he is certainly better than most of the thirdraters on the actual scene. Such men as Penrose and Lodge are sorely missed when Republicans now come together. Their places have been taken by puerile wind-jammers of the Simeon D. Fess variety, and by gross and crude manipulators of the caliber of Robert H. Lucas and James Francis Burke. A Republican national convention used to be very high-toned. It almost suggested an assembly of the League of Nations. But now it is cheap and shabby, and the more intelligent the leader who pops up, the less likely he is to do any real leading. In the present case the whole thing is being run from the White House, which has the usual difficulty in making up its mind.

Chicago has apparently laid in enough supplies to keep all the wets well oiled and even to take the edge off the thirst of the unhappy drys, but the prices quoted by the town booticians seem excessive to Eastern visitors. Gin of a grade which brings from $5 to $6 a gallon in Baltimore is here vended for as much as $35 a case, which works out to $14.50 a gallon. Decent Scotch costs from $8 to $10 a bottle, with the twelfth bottle thrown in free if one buys a whole case. Canadian Bourbon costs from $5 to $6 a pint, or $30 a half dozen pints. Better Scotch is selling in Baltimore at $60 a case and in New York at $55 or $58, and Bourbon just as good goes for $48 a dozen quarts, not pints.

Even beer is very expensive. The ordinary Canadian brews, which now sell in Baltimore for $6 a case of twenty-four bottles, cost $12 here. The local product, which grades down from a wishy-washy *Helles* to an almost undrinkable bilge, brings from $5 to $7 a case. These prices are causing a widespread lifting of eyebrows, for most of the visitors came to town expecting to find beer flowing like water and at very neat prices. Moreover, figuring that Canada was only across the street, they counted on filling themselves with hard liquor at a cost considerably below the common level. But it is not so, alas, alas.

The booticians put the blame upon what they call, with polite euphemism, the syndicate. This syndicate, though the Capones are behind the bars, is still functioning powerfully, and its main purpose seems to be to keep up profits. The retailers are left only a small margin, and so they cannot cut prices materially. If they protest, their supplies are withdrawn altogether and their business is ruined. A few of the bolder among them sometimes turn to outlaw bootleggers, who run the stuff in from Canada by motor boat and are content with more modest profits. But any speakeasy operator who is known to dally with such bootleggers is apt to have his place bombed and his head cracked, to say the least. For the syndicate believes in Law Enforcement, and it enforces its own laws much more effectively than the Prohibition agents enforce those of the State and nation.

The cops in Chicago have been getting their wages only irregularly for several months past. Not infrequently, when their pay-day comes round, it turns out that there is not enough money in the depleted city treasury to pay them. Thus a good many of them have been thrown for support upon the speakeasy proprietors, some of whom have been allowing every cop within sight of their doors $5 a week. But now some of the speakeasy men, knowing that they have the cops at their mercy, have begun to cut down this dole, and the poor gendarmes are on a hot spot. They will probably linger upon it until the city is restored to complete solvency, which may be a long while. There is much public sympathy for them in their time of trouble, for being a cop in Chicago is not an easy job, and most members of the force are fine fellows.

The Chicago taste in stimulants, to a cultivated Easterner, seems somewhat primitive. Beer is drunk generally, but beyond it one hears of little save Scotch and Bourbon. Even rye seems to be only moderately esteemed. I was told by several persons active in the illicit liquor business that still wines have practically no market in the town and that even champagne is fast going out of fashion. Nor is there much demand for cordials, which are drunk heavily in the New York speakeasies, especially by women clients.

All of this seems strange to a visitor from the seaboard, for the booters there offer a great variety of drinkables, even including vintage wines. Very fair Sauternes are now selling in New York at $35 a case, and excellent Rhines and Moselles are obtainable at from $45 to $60. Practically every brand of Scotch ever heard of in Scotland is on sale, and there is a rich and copious supply of brandies and liqueurs. But Chicago contents itself with far fewer gems. It has the quantity, but cannot match New York and Baltimore when it comes to quality. This, however, is not ruinous during a national convention. Politicians, in general, are not fastidious, and most of those from the interior, especially the drys, are ready to drink anything that burns, at the same time giving thanks to God.

III

THE CLOWNS ENTER
THE RING

[From the Baltimore Evening Sun, June 14, 1932]

Chicago, June 14

TOWARD NOON the twentieth Republican National Convention got under way at last, with the usual brief moments of glory for nonentities. For fifteen minutes before the gavel actually fell, the Hon. Simeon D. Fess, the Ohio pedagogue, posed with it in his hand, blinking in 100,000 candlepower of light, with a dozen cameras and movie machines aimed at his bald head. Fess has been in politics now for years, but he was a gogue for so long that the chalk is still on his hands, and so he could not resist the chance to loose an harangue on the American flag, full of old-time Third Reader stuff. He also quarreled with the light men, who continued to shoot at his bald head, and otherwise let it be known that he was somebody, if only for a short space, and would not tolerate any invasion of his prerogative. He concluded with the pledge to the flag that poor school children are forced to memorize, at the same time throwing out what remains of his chest.

There ensued a couple of speeches by local worthies, and then uprose Bishop James E. Freeman of Washington to ask divine approval of the proceedings. How Bishop Freeman, who is an Episcopalian, got the job that belonged by every right to Bishop James Cannon, Jr., did not appear. He prayed briefly and in an humble spirit, but as his words were flung out in thunderous volume by the loud speakers they sounded almost like indignation. He was followed by one George DeBenneville Keim, of New Jersey, who, so it appeared, is secretary of the Republican National Committee. DeBenneville read the call for the convention in a hurried, gargling manner, and then slunk back into that black obscurity whence, for his hundred seconds, he had emerged.

THE CLOWNS ENTER THE RING

Then Professor Fess dragged out the keynoter, Senator L. J. Dickinson, of Algona, Iowa, and the convention was under sail. It was then six minutes after noon. The galleries were scarcely more than half full. Dickinson is an old-time political hack of the cow State model, and has only recently risen to the dizzy eminence of a United States Senator. He howled his canned speech in a loud and hearty manner, and with frequent gestures and shakes of his bushy head. At the end of his seventh sentence he pronounced the awful name of Hoover and there was a halt for applause. It lasted a minute and a half.

During all of these opening ceremonies the Machiavellian ex-Senator Joseph I. France, M.D., of Maryland, sat in a front seat in the speaker's stand, and mulled his immoral scheme to stop Hoover and grab the nomination himself. During the praying of Bishop Freeman, Dr. France kept his eyes shut tightly, bowed his head, and heaved in silent sympathy with the prayer. He arose, too, when Fess recited the flag pledge, and when the Republican Glee Club of Columbus, Ohio, sang "The Star-Spangled Banner." But when Dickinson mentioned Hoover, France kept his seat, chewed gum in a defiant manner, and permitted a cynical smile to irradiate his face. There is wickedness in his heart. He will fetch Hoover or bust.[1]

Dickinson roared along for the better part of an hour. He spoke so fast and the loud speakers made such a din of his words that no one could follow him. Whenever he halted for breath and looked up expectantly the delegates and alternates applauded formally, but they made quite as much noise over his statement that pessimism was lately rampant in the world as over the news that Hoover single handed had saved Europe. He went far too fast to heat them up. It takes a slower and more oleaginous approach to shake a crowd so large. In the main, the speech of the hon. gentleman was made up of the dismal blather that is always discharged on such occasions. No one in the hall could make out what most of it was about.

[1] Dr. France served in the United States Senate from Maryland from 1917 to 1923. He showed Progressive tendencies, opposed the Wilson *cheka*, and always voted wet. In the Spring of 1932 he entered various Republican primaries, and carried four or five States against Hoover. He came to Chicago convinced that he could stop Hoover and get the nomination himself. What happened to him is told in one of the dispatches dated June 16.

THE CLOWNS ENTER THE RING

The delegates and alternates, apparently quite devoid of any curiosity about it, sat through it on their hard chairs, reading newspapers, smoking in violation of the Chicago fire laws, and patiently scratching themselves. Toward the end they began stretching, shuffling their feet and visiting about, and Professor Fess reappeared to bang for order. After that Dickinson howled louder and louder, but the louder he hooted the worse the hash that the loud speakers made of his rhetoric.

As incredible as it may seem, there was not a syllable in his speech about Prohibition, the one subject that the delegates have been talking about since they came to town. He did not allude to it even indirectly. There was not the slightest hint in all his roaring that great hordes of resolute wets sat before him, and that they would be making a desperate effort this very afternoon to get a wet plank into the party platform. He was sounding the party keynote and yet he avoided completely the one question really before the house, the party and the country.

But such unrealities always mark a Republican national convention. It is, in its normal form, a kind of grotesque fairy play, enacted by one-legged, wooden-headed and preposterous marionettes. This time it is even worse than usual, for most of the more competent party leaders are detained at Washington, and the show is in charge of such selling-platers as Dickinson and Fess. Thus the whole thing becomes a hollow buffoonery and until orders are received from the White House the proceedings will continue on the level of a game of I-spy played by half-witted children.

At the conclusion of the keynote speech some one set up a cheer and it lasted for precisely eleven seconds. The delegates and alternates arose politely and most of the dignitaries on the platform joined them. But not Dr. France of Maryland. His sinister enmity to Lord Hoover continued to consume him and he sat firmly in his place, at work upon his second package of chewing gum and with a fiendish sneer upon his face. Presently one of his secret agents down on the floor caught his eye and gave the Fascist salute. He is watched carefully by the Hoover sleuth, Signor Richey *geb*. Ricci, and by the bomb squad of the Chicago *gendarmerie*.

THE CLOWNS ENTER THE RING

After this the proceedings petered out, and the delegates began to return to their hotels. Various secretaries arose to make various unintelligible announcements, and in some unknown manner the committees on platform, credentials and rules were appointed. At four o'clock this afternoon the battle over the platform will begin in one of the gaudy parlors of the Congress Hotel. The first session adjourned at 1.20. The second will begin at eleven o'clock tomorrow morning.

God save the Republic!

IV

THE LAST STAND OF THE DRYS

[From the Baltimore Evening Sun, June 15, 1932]

Chicago, June 15

THIS CONVENTION of country postmasters, Federal marshals and receivers in bankruptcy, masquerading as the heirs of Lincoln, is the stupidest and most boresome ever heard of; nevertheless, it will probably get its paragraph in the history books, for it is witnessing the death struggles of Prohibition. If the delegates were really free agents they would vote the imposture out by a majority of at least five to one. They quibble and compromise only because such is the word that comes from Washington. But even that compromise is a dreadful defeat for the drys, and they know it. Four years ago they would have cracked their whip and sent Lord Hoover sailing through their hoop like an arrow. But now he heaves and blunders through the air like a doormat, and half of him lands inside and half outside.

The whole sad drama was played out in miniature at the hearing before the resolutions committee yesterday afternoon. Approaching the parlor in the Congress Hotel where it was held, I found a sweating, fuming crowd milling around the closed doors, and was amazed to discover Bishop James Cannon, Jr., in the midst of it. He greeted me pleasantly, but it was plain to see that he was very unhappy. And no wonder! Try to imagine Bishop Cannon waiting outside the door of Republican politicians four years ago! Or even a year ago! But there he lingered for a bad half hour, elbowed horribly by wet cuties with huge repeal banners flapping across their façades, and when he was admitted at last the committee did not even hear him.

The contrast with the scene at Houston four years ago was really most pathetic. There the bishop and his allies faced a frankly hostile candidate in Al Smith, who was notoriously in favor of a dripping wet platform. But they beat him down in the resolutions committee, and put through a platform precisely to their taste, and Al was reduced to the perilous device of repealing and reënacting it with his own amendments. But this year the tide is roaring the other way, and the best they can get, even in the house of their friends, is a disingenuous and preposterous straddle.

They made a good fight before the resolutions committee, and put forward some of their most effective argufiers—Ernest H. Cherrington, Daniel A. Poling, F. Scott McBride, Col. Raymond Robbins and the saintly Mrs. Ella A. Boole, grand goblin of the W. C. T. U. They even produced a pretty and well-dressed young woman —a Mrs. Rushman Patterson, of Washington— the most sightly creature, and by long odds, ever witnessed by these eyes on the dry side of the fence. But the wets had orators just as adept and lady supporters even more pulchritudinous and, morever, destiny was plainly with them. They had all of the assurance. They were full of a contagious confidence. The battle was going their way. The drys fought gamely, but it was without any visible hope.

Even the bishop was scarcely himself. He told me that he would go on fighting to the last ditch, and I believed him, but I observed that he said nothing whatever about winning. The other dry spokesman took the same cautious line. They admitted freely that the opposition to Prohibition was formidable, and that it was growing. They talked frankly of a time when it might be necessary, and even advisable, to put the whole thing to another test at the polls. All they ventured to plead for was the kind of test provided for by Article V of the Constitution, and at least one of them, Colonel Robbins, admitted categorically that they favored this plan because it would give the dry side a great advantage, and that without that advantage they would probably lose.

All of which, I confess, was music to my ears. I could not help recalling the many other occasions when I had heard the same apostles do their stuff, or refrain from contrasting their old cockiness with their present despairs. It was pleasant to see them palpably licked, but it was also somewhat sad. Here were the most accomplished political manipulators ever on display in the America of my time, and now they were brought down at last and their old enemies were gloating over them. They still have some good fights in them, and the formal clearing off of the Prohibition rubbish will probably be a long and difficult business, but there can be no doubt hereafter that it will be cleared off.

The scene of the dry Waterloo was a garish parlor in the convention headquarters hotel— the sort of apartment in which Rotarians blow their spitballs and brass-band weddings are staged. At one end was a long table for the officers of the resolutions committee, with the excessively polite Dr. James R. Garfield, its chairman, in the center. Dr. Garfield gave each side half an hour and banged his gavel the instant time was up. For the wets Pierre S. du Pont was floor manager, and for the drys Dr. Cherrington. Each operated by pulling coattails. There was very little applause for either side.

In front of the chairman's place were a couple of rows of chairs for members of the committee and behind them a few more rows for the more eminent and infirm among the wets and drys. They were thrown together indiscriminately. The celebrated Canon Chase of Brooklyn was flanked by two wet sweeties and on the other side Dr. Nicholas Murray Butler found himself cheek by jowl with Dr. McBride. The chairs filled less than half the room. The rest of the space was for standees. They sweated painfully, for the day was hot. Tobacco smoke filled the air.

A dozen or more newspaper photographers, including a Jap, set off flashlights at intervals of ten or fifteen seconds. When a speaker came forward to address the committee they closed in on him and shot him from all four sides. Sometimes they made so much noise that the proceedings had to be halted to clear them off. They always came back. Thus the drys fought their last great fight, with smoke strangling them and flashlights blinding them.

As I have said, the scene was full of melancholy. These were tough babies, and in their day they had drawn buckets of blood. I have seen some of the most eminent statesmen in America blanch at their frown. They put Hoover into the White House and kept Al out. They once owned all the State Legislatures, hoof and hide. They still own a working majority in Congress. But it is fading. Every day another serf throws off his shackles. The poor dogs are licked.

Their last bite, I suspect, is reserved for Lord Hoover. He has saved them from complete disaster, but only to make it certain on some near tomorrow. What they will do about it I don't know, but it is obvious that the old love affair is near its end. Mrs. Boole, in her speech, hinted that many of them, next November, will stay away from the polls. But a good many others will probably vote for the Democrat—provided he is wet enough. For in their present low mood they have far more inclination toward an open enemy than toward a false friend.

V

THE WETS SWING INTO THE SADDLE

[From the Baltimore Evening Sun, June 16, 1932]

Chicago, June 16

THE GREAT combat over Prohibition, though it kept the delegates sweating in their stalls until nearly two o'clock this morning and has left them woozy and unhappy today, was really only a sham battle. For the fighting was not between the wets and drys; it was simply between two factions of wets. The first, led by Senator Hiram Bingham of Connecticut and Dr. Nicholas Murray Butler, was in favor of a forthright and unequivocal repudiation of the whole Prohibition imposture. The second, led by Lord Hoover's agents, fought for temporizing and compromise. That compromise, according to the belief of the Hoover men today, is sufficiently subtle and confusing to fool the beaten drys, but I find myself quite unable to believe that they are such suckers. The thing they actually advocated was the old Law Enforcement buncombe, and when they discovered that it was lost they virtually abandoned the fight.

During the long debate last night they put up only one speaker, and he had such a brief hearing that he could not state their case. All of the other orators, whether they spoke for the official plank or the Butler substitute, were plainly against Prohibition, and the most they asked the convention to do was to avoid ruining Hoover by coming out for immediate and unconditional repeal. Consider, for example, the case of the Hon. Ogden L. Mills, the chief Administration spokesman. Mills, as everyone knows, is one of the wettest wets in Washington. For months he has been trying to induce Lord Hoover to abandon the lost cause. He is so wet that, put beside him, even Dr. Butler begins to look a bit parched. And yet this same Mills was not only told off to fashion the Administration plank on the subject, but was also put up to defend it! He defended it very stoutly and in a voice of brass, but the most he could say in favor of Prohibition was that it ought to be got rid of in a deliberate and orderly way, and without heaving all the really dry States to the mercies of the breweries.

The question now is, what will the drys do about it? They know very well that they have got a dreadful beating, but they are still good enough politicians to try to snatch some advantage out of defeat. The more extreme fanatics among them, led by Mrs. Henry W. Peabody, formerly of wet Massachusetts and now of wet Florida,[1] are already planning to call an anti-Hoover conference at Indianapolis on July 4, and many of the heartbroken W. C. T. U. ladies, according to their leader, Mrs. Ella Boole, will not vote at all. But the more practical drys of the so-called Board of Strategy are still hunting for a place to head in, and some of them seem to believe that the Democrats will provide it for them.

The Democrats, in fact, will have a hard time framing a plank that is less consolatory to drys

[1] This unfortunate lady moved out of Massachusetts because it was too wet for her. She chose Florida as her refuge, but she had scarcely got there before it too went wet.

than that upon which Hoover will stand. If they go an inch further they will have to come out for immediate and outright repeal, and that is something that the Southern lynchers and Bible students will oppose to the last ditch. Thus it begins to look probable that the Democratic plank, when it is put together at last with split boards and rusty nails, will be not wetter than the Hoover plank, and there is even a fair chance that it may be a shade more dry.[2] On this possibility the dry grand goblins put their remaining hopes. If they can alarm the Democrats into listening to them, they will be able to punish Hoover for his treason. If not, they will walk out and leave the whole sad business to the jurisprudence of a just and wrathful God.

Last night's bout in the stadium was a sort of gaudy *reductio ad absurdum* of the whole process of government under democracy. For nearly five hours thousands of men and women, all of them theoretically chosen because of their special interest in and talent for statecraft, howled and roared over a sham battle, and meanwhile

[2] I do not apologize for this error. Not a soul in Chicago, on June 16, dreamed that the Democrats would actually tear up their official plank and go the whole hog.

all of the grave and desperate problems confronting the country went unconsidered and even un-
mentioned. Everyone was well aware all the while
that sufficient Federal jobholders would be
rounded up in the end to save the Hoover plank,
and yet speaker after speaker fulminated against
it as if its fate were actually at issue. And when,
at last, it was put to a vote, hundreds voted for it
who were notoriously against it.

The one thing that the uproar demonstrated
was the overwhelming importance of Prohibition. The leaders of the convention made every
effort to put it in a pocket and so get rid of it,
but it burst out irresistibly and swept every other
question out of consideration. The platform
planks dealing with those other questions went
unregarded and even unheard. While Dr. James
R. Garfield, chairman of the committee on resolutions, droned them into the microphone the
delegates shuffled about the hall, scarcely hearing a word. Nothing that he had to say was chal-
lenged and nothing was applauded. But the moment he reached the Prohibition plank the whole
hall was alert, and, thereafter, for three hours
every syllable of every speaker was heard with

attention, and the interruptions were frequent and noisy.

The debate went on in the theatrical and even fantastic atmosphere which now characterizes national conventions. There used to be a time when genuine orators addressed such gatherings, and even the most puerile doctrine was given a certain dignity by grand and voluptuous words. But now all voices come out of the loud speakers on the same huge scale, and there is no more difference between one and another than between two explosions of dynamite. Meanwhile, the speaker himself has become no more than a piece of stage property for the photographers and movie men.

They turn immense lights upon him, blinding and rattling him. They rush up upon him in the midst of his most solemn periods and bang away at him with flashes. They yell to him to move over, to stop a minute, to do it again. The whole thing is unimaginably undignified, ludicrous and obscene, and it must be painful for speakers of any dignity and self-respect. But the professional politicians, of course, enjoy it. Such professionals are running the present convention, and most of them are of a very low order. There is an almost complete absence of really salient and interesting personalities among them. Dr. Nicholas Murray Butler, to be sure, is above the common run, but he is growing old, and everything that he has to say has been heard before. Senator Bingham has a great deal of energy, but he makes a rather feeble speech, and his prancing somehow gives the impression that he is rather too well pleased with himself. On the other side the chief master minds are members of the Hoover Cabinet, but only one of them shows any noticeable superiority to a police sergeant, and that one has had the horrible job of piloting Hoover across the shell-torn No Man's Land between the wet and dry armies.

I have seen many conventions, but this one is the worst. It is both the stupidest and the most dishonest. Its decisions are reached for puerile reasons and it is led by quacks. The one thing that gives it any intellectual dignity is its frank recognition of the overmastering importance of Prohibition as an issue. It has not wasted any time gabbling about world courts, farmers' relief, and other such banshees, but has given over its whole time and thought to the one great question of questions. But even on that question it has not been really candid. When the roll was called this morning at least 700 of the delegates in the hall were in favor of repeal, and probably a full half of them were in favor of the return of the saloon. But only 472 voted for the Butler amendment, and even the Butler amendment gave the saloon a kick.

Consider, for example, the Maryland delegation. Bound by the idiotic unit rule, it cast its nineteen votes for the Hoover compromise, and so held the Free State up to shame and ignominy. Only two members of the delegation had the courage to serve public notice that they were actually for repeal. And yet a fair poll of the delegation, taken in secret, would probably show at least fifteen votes for repeal, and nine or ten for the old-time saloon, with five-cent schooners on the bar, landscapes done in soap on the mirror behind it, a large hand-painted oil painting of Venus rising from the bath on the opposite wall, and a sound free lunch of potato salad, embalmed celery and prehistoric *Blutwurst* on a side table.

THE WETS IN THE SADDLE

If Federal jobholders have gone so far, imagine how far the rest of the American people have gone. Prohibition has suddenly fallen over like a house of cards. A year ago, even six months ago, the drys were still full of confidence, for they were sure that they had Lord Hoover in their cage. But he has broken out, slipped off his nose ring, and headed for the bad lands. The one remaining hope of the brethren lies in the Democrats. On that side of the fence politics is usually practised as a branch of suicide. But this time even the Democrats may refuse to jump.

—VI—

INTERLUDE:
THE BUM'S RUSH FOR A
PROGRESSIVE

[From the Baltimore Evening Sun, June 16, 1932]

Chicago, June 16

FORMER SENATOR Joseph I. France of Maryland got his day in court at last today, but it was over in five minutes, and it came near costing him a cracked head.

The sonorous Mr. L. B. Sandblast of Oregon had just finished a long and dull speech putting his name before the convention when Dr. France himself appeared upon the platform, a paper in his hand. He was moving toward the loud speakers when Chairman Bertrand H. Snell halted him, and there was a sudden hush in the hall when it was seen that they were engaged in an angry colloquy. France struggled to get to the desk and Snell tried to hold him back. France would have won, for he is much larger than Snell, but before he could advance more than a few steps a couple of assistant sergeants-at-arms rushed up. And there began a rough struggle.

It was over in half a minute. France tried hard to shake himself loose, but the sergeants-at-arms were quickly joined by a squad of Chicago cops, and the man whose name had just been put before the convention went out as the center of a bum's rush. Meanwhile the delegates and alternates got to their feet and the whole hall was in turmoil. Few of the spectators knew who France was. And none knew what he was trying to do. The cops ran him out through the stand across the lobby to the rear and upstairs to their temporary bastile on the second floor. A hundred newspaper correspondents and photographers followed after, and the flashlights began to explode. The rumor went about that a crazy man had broken upon the platform and tried to butcher Snell.

But once he reached the stadium hoosegow France turned out to be very far from insane. At once he got upon a table and addressed the cops and correspondents who crowded about him.

"What were you doing on the platform?" some one demanded.

"I was there to nominate Calvin Coolidge of Massachusetts."

"Are you a delegate?"

"No, but I have a proxy from Oregon."

"Then you were about to withdraw yourself?"

"Exactly. I was going to put Coolidge in nomination and if they had let me do it he'd have swept the convention."

"What do you mean by they?"

"The gang running this convention. You see now what sort of people they are. They knew what I was up to and they were determined to shut me off. They violated the rules of the convention to do so and they violated every rule of fair play and common honesty."

"Did Snell know that you had a proxy?"

"I told him as I came upon the platform. The secretary had reached Oregon in the call of the roll. I had been put in nomination by Mr. Sandblast. But Oregon still had the floor, and I had a clear right to be heard. I want the country to know what a bunch is running the Republican party. You have seen for yourself. I expected that they would try to shut me off, but I didn't think they would have me thrown out by the police."

The cops, in fact, handled Dr. France very gently and there were no signs of trauma upon him. The police captain in charge of the bum's rush apologized for it.

"I was only obeying orders," he protested, when he heard that his prisoner was a former United States Senator.

"Stupid orders," replied Dr. France.

Before he could start a speech the photographers closed in on him and began banging their flashlights at him. He posed for them with his clenched fist raised aloft and an indignant frown on his face. But he seemed to be in very good humor, and when the radio men came rushing up and offering him time on the air he accepted with alacrity. The cops said that they had no charge to lodge against him. Russell Hawkins, of Portland, chairman of the Oregon delegation, issued this statement:

"I gave Senator France his authority. The

transaction was also duly authorized by all the delegates who signed the form. The name of Alternate France was not on the form, which was in blank when it was signed, but this morning the delegates were duly informed that he was an alternate. I called Bob Williams, our national committeeman, and informed him of my action. France had a right to the floor and had a right to be heard."

THE REPUBLICANS
GO HOME

[From the Baltimore Evening Sun, June 17, 1932]

Chicago, June 17

EVEN FEDERAL jobholders, when it comes to Prohibition, are now hard to hold in line. They came perilously near to rejecting the Hoover platform straddle on Wednesday night, and they gave old Charlie Curtis a serious scare yesterday afternoon. The attack on the straddle did not come from the drys, for they were all convinced that it was the best they could hope for, but from the wets. And the raid upon old Charlie was conducted from the same quarter, and the chief consideration behind it was not that Charlie was too old for another term, or too horribly stupid and preposterous, but simply that he was too dry. If a really attractive wet had got into the struggle for second place, he would have been nominated without a doubt. But all the wets had to fight with were a couple of war heroes, and neither was good enough to turn the trick. Bert Snell might have had the nomination, but he was too wise.

The extent of the wet revolt in the Republican party is really most amazing. When it was first heard of, a year or so ago, it seemed to be confined to a few big city politicians who could be trusted, when the test came, to turn as dry as Lord Hoover demanded. But by the time the delegates to the convention got to Chicago it was obvious that the thing had gone very much further than that, and Hoover's agents bombarded him with warnings that he would have to shin down the Anti-Saloon League pole. He did so as gracefully as possible, but it was not enough. Fully a half of the delegates wanted to go the whole hog, and even when the heaviest sort of pressure was brought to bear upon them two-fifths voted for the Butler amendment.

The revolt was mainly in the North and Middle West. The white and black delegates from the

THE REPUBLICANS GO HOME

South, where job-holding is almost the only occupation of Republicans, obeyed the orders of the White House without question, and are thus sure of cornmeal and hog meat next Winter. But in the delegations from above the Potomac even the postmasters and United States marshals refused to stay in the Anti-Saloon League pen, and as a result the count actually showed more votes among them against the Hoover compromise than for it. Certainly this was a marvel that deserved all the black headlines it got. Two years ago, or even a year ago, it would have seemed a sheer impossibility. But now it has come to pass.

The Republicans are going home today in a frame of mind that is anything but exultant. They are aware that Mr. Hoover has failed to win back the public esteem that he never really had, and that he remains one of the most unpopular Presidents on record. And they are uneasy about the attitude of the drys to the Hoover plank, once there is a chance to think it over. Many of the dry bosses, to be sure, show signs of falling in step, but what is going on among the country Bible students is still undetermined. If they are even dumber than anyone has ever suspected they will accept the Hoover plank as a victory for Prohibition. But if there is any trace of common sense in them, they will see that they have been hornswoggled, and their wrath will fall where it belongs.

The one real hope of the Republican leaders lies in the probability that the Democrats, when they meet on June 27, will be divided even more seriously, and that whatever compromise they reach will be worse. The Hoover plank at least has the great virtue of being quite unintelligible to simple folk. Even the specialists here on the scene continue to dispute about it. I sat yesterday with four experts of mature years and endless experience, and yet they debated for an hour as to whether the plank will bring a quick test of Prohibition and a quick end of it, or an indefinite postponement of the whole matter. In the Bible country uncertainty will be doubly damned, and the faithful will probably believe anything their pastors choose to tell them.

But if the Democrats come out with a plank that is short and easily understood, and especially if they come out with one that says substantially what the Hoover plank is thought to say, then the clouds that now hang about the Republican sky will begin to clear. For then it will be relatively easy for the Republicans to hold the backwoods in line. Such hopes and surmises, of course, must remain vague until the Democrats actually do their stuff, but experience shows that they are seldom equal to such a chance as now confronts them. If they would come out for repeal and nominate a thumping wet they might send Lord Hoover flying back to Australia, but that is precisely what a good many of their master minds will not let them do if it can be helped.

The more I see of conventions the more I marvel that anyone can be induced to attend them. They offer, at intervals, a thoroughly good show, at least in the sense that seeing an elderly cripple fall on the ice and break his remaining leg is a good show, but the waits between are very long and tiresome. Last night more than 10,000 people sat on hard chairs for four hours while a depressing succession of bad speakers roared into the microphone. This oratory was bad almost beyond description, but it must have been measurably less bad over the radio, with a comfortable chair to sit in and a cold bottle of home brew on the side table.

The business of a national convention is always carried on in the most tedious and wasteful way imaginable. It is not sufficient that a chairman should be elected to police the proceedings. He must be elected twice, in the persons of two different men, and both of them must be permitted to make long and unintelligible speeches. No resolution can be passed in the ordinary parliamentary manner. It must be proposed in all solemnity by a neighborhood magnifico fetched to the platform for the purpose, and the vote upon it must be taken with the elaborate ceremony of a baptism by total immersion. At least two hundred windjammers are on hand, panting for their turns in the glaring lights, and soon or late all of them must be accommodated. Whoever is not noticed by the photographers goes home with a broken heart, and broken hearts count on the wrong side on election day.

The whole thing is simply an elaborate scheme for wasting time and money. Too many delegates are elected, and too many of them are mere blanks. A gathering of a hundred, or even of two hundred, reasonably sensible men and women could select the two candidates in an hour, adopt a short platform in another hour, and have the rest of the day left to visit the speakeasies. But instead of a hundred there are more than a thousand, and instead of the few officers who suffice for an ordinary meeting there are hordes of bombastic and futile functionaries, all of them the most stupid and degraded sort of political hacks. And the proceedings are dragged on for long days and nights simply and solely to give a gang of slightly superior mountebanks a chance to posture and perform. Not one man out of forty who addresses a national convention has anything worth hearing to say, and not one in twenty is worth seeing and meeting for any other reason.

The Republicans who are going home today, some of them by train, but more of them by bus, leave Chicago regretting them very little. They gave a poor show and spent relatively little money. In these hard times the old gouging is impossible, and in consequence hotel rates here have been very moderate. But outside their board and lodging the visitors apparently bought next to nothing. Certainly the speakeasies enjoyed no rush of patronage, and equally certainly the hotel booticians were not overworked. It was, all in all, a very poor convention. Chicago hopes for something better from the Democrats, but it is not too sure.

—VIII—

THE DRYS NURSE THEIR WOUNDS

[From the Baltimore Evening Sun, June 18, 1932]

Chicago, June 18

THAT THE historic events of the past week have put the professional Prohibitionists on a hot spot seems to be generally believed, but there is still room for dispute as to how hot that spot really is. The treason of Lord Hoover was bad enough, but the falling away of such fat cats as John D. Rockefeller, Jr., Alfred P. Sloan, Jr., president of General Motors, and Harvey Firestone is a good deal worse, for Hoover was always a liability as well as an asset, whereas Rockefeller and company represented only cash money of the highest standard of weight and fineness. But now that money begins to be cut off, and the dry apostles look forward to a meager Winter. In the South, where their best pastures are, the defection of Rockefeller means more than mere loss of *mazuma*, for he is venerated down there as the leading Baptist extant, and so he is likely to be imitated, not only by Babbitts, but also by multitudes of the lowly.

Nevertheless, the future is not altogether black for the dry wizards, for plenty of irreconcilable drys remain, and there is a lot of new fuel for heating them up. The Hoover infamy, for the moment, paralyzes these faithful ones, but they will be coming back. If, in his speeches during the campaign, the fallen angel grows wetter and wetter, then there will be all the more reason for them to stand pat. And if, as seems more likely, he throws them a few bones, then they will gather fresh enthusiasm. In either case there will be a clarion call for their leaders to operate on them, and no one doubts that, when that call comes, those leaders will respond.

The money question is the most pressing. The Anti-Saloon League is already next door to bankruptcy, and the other dry organizations are all short of funds. In the last campaign Bishop Cannon found a gold mine in the mysterious Mr. Jameson, and Jameson paid most of the bills until the Republican politicians began to respond. But this year it will be hard to find a Jameson, and tapping the Republican war-chest will be difficult, for most of the big contributors are wringing wet and have already served notice that none of their money is to be used for promoting Prohibition. Thus the bishop has his troubles, and is saying very little. His silence during the Republican convention was excused on the ground that he is a Democrat, but when the Democrats meet week after next they are surely not likely to embrace him as one of them. If you know of any well-heeled fellow who believes that Prohibition is wise and can be saved and enforced, it would be an act of Christian decency to send his name to the Rt. Rev. James Cannon, Jr., D. D., Bliss Building, Washington, D. C. Even anonymous tips will be appreciated.

Mr. Hoover is also on a hot spot, but he has been on so many since he took office that one more will probably not incommode him. It will be hard for him to discuss Prohibition during the campaign, and it will be almost impossible for him to avoid it. For the Republican plank is so full of words and so vague in important places that an angry debate about its precise meaning is bound to arise, and if he ducks that debate he will do as much damage as if he engages in it. His difficulty lies in the fact that all of his chief advisers are wet, and that they insist that the platform plank is wet, too. If he agrees with them, the surviving drys will be twice as sore as they are now, and if he tries to straddle again, then both sides will be against him.

As I said yesterday, the chief Republican hope today lies in the probability that the Democrats will have a long drawn out and bloody battle over Prohibition, and that they will also try to compromise in the end. Republicans have a natural talent for compromise, but to Democrats it is almost impossible. Thus if they avoid the danger of coming out either too wet or too dry, they will probably concoct a bad imitation of the Republican straddle, baffling and irritating to all hands. Moreover, they have a bitter fight for the nomination on their hands, and before they finish with it they will probably be in a very low and ragged state.

The drys were not surprised by the Hoover maneuver, and, being realists, they did not pretend to be surprised. Most of them had become convinced some time ago that Hoover would certainly walk out on them if he were reëlected, and many of them believed that he would do so as soon as he was renominated. I don't believe they are really angry with him, for as practical politicians they know that he really couldn't help himself. They can see as well as anyone that Prohibition is on the toboggan, and they realize that if he had not yielded to the inflamed and resolute wets he'd have had a first-rate revolt on his hands. Even so, the wets gave him a serious scare, and after the main bout was over they came near taking out their accumulated bile on poor old Charley Curtis, the dry Indian.

The really important result of the convention is that hundreds of Republican politicians are going home convinced that it is all over with Prohibition. They will spread the news where it will count. A great many Republican statesmen are already over the fence, and others are making quiet leaps daily. The drys have their backs to the wall. They are daring and resourceful fighters, and there is still one more big battle in them, but fortune has plainly deserted them, and they seem to be doomed.

AFTERMATH [1]

[From the Baltimore Evening Sun, June 20, 1932]

Chicago, June 19

IT IS too soon to hear what interpretation Lord Hoover himself reads into the resubmission plank adopted by his lieges last Wednesday, if indeed he has any interpretation to offer, and too soon to get any certain light and leading from the prelates of the State church, now in process of disestablishment. Hoover will keep mum upon the subject as long as he can, and maybe that will be clear up to election day. There is nothing in his make-up demanding frankness. He prefers to

[1] This article appeared on the editorial page of the *Evening Sun*. I print an article there every Monday afternoon, and have been doing so for years.

dodge whenever he can, which is usually. As for the prelates, they wait uneasily for the Democratic plank. The final choice before them, they now see, will not be between wetness and dryness, as they hoped up to a week ago, but between two kinds of wetness. They must find out which is the wetter before they let it be known what God has to say in the premises.

Most of them, I suspect, now hope and believe that it will be possible for them to support Hoover in the campaign. They will, of course, demand loudly that next week's Democratic convention keep its hands off the Eighteenth Amendment, and they will get a certain amount of support from Bible students among the delegates, but they now know very well that the party plank will be at least as wet as the Republican plank, and that the standard-bearer, whoever he is, will be far wetter than Hoover. Thus they will be thrown back on the Great Engineer, their hero of yesteryear, and in the interval they refrain prudently from saying anything about him that may incommode them hereafter.

He is, in fact, their kind of man, and they do not forget his high services to the holy cause in

the past. Officially he is a Quaker, but he has a
Methodist mind. When the Wickersham Report
started Prohibition down the toboggan he came
to the bat with a hearty denunciation of repeal,
and on all other occasions he has done the best
he could, considering his situation and his character, to play the apostles' game. They are not
really angry with him for yielding to the embat-
tled wets last Wednesday. They know he couldn't
help himself, and they are grateful to him for at
least beating the Butler plank. If he had not sent
his spies and jackals to the front the convention
would have turned into a wet camp-meeting,
shouting hallelujahs like a convention of Elks.

But beating the Butler plank, though it was a
feat of politics, was scarcely a victory of policy,
for the two planks, in all essentials, were iden-
tical. Both demanded an immediate resubmission of Prohibition, and both demanded that it
be resubmitted, not to the State Legislatures,
which the drys might manage to control, but to
"State conventions called for that sole purpose,"
which would be much harder to handle. Even in
the sops that they threw to the poor drys the two
planks were substantially alike, for both included

rhetorical flings at the saloon, and both pledged
the party to support measures aimed at rigid
control of the liquor traffic and at the promotion
of temperance. The only vital difference between
them lay in the fact that the Butler plank advocated repeal, whereas the official plank stopped
at resubmission.

But only a little reflection is needed to show
that this difference was, and is, of small practical importance. The Prohibitionists know very
well that, if the question is allowed to go to
the people, the popular vote will show an immense wet majority, and that if they attempt
to nullify that majority by rigging the manner in which delegates to the conventions are
elected they will probably lose more than they
gain. What they face is an urgent and ever-
increasing popular demand that the whole Prohibition imposture be got rid of. They fought
desperately to prevent the question going before
the people, and they have been beaten all along
the line.

The details are unimportant: the main thing is
that they have been turned out of their constitu-
tional citadel and forced to accept battle in the

open. Nor is it important that the Republican plank stops short of calling for immediate repeal, for everyone knows that repeal and resubmission are one and the same—that every honest call for resubmission has come from wets, not from drys. What the drys tried to do was to shelve the whole matter—to make it impossible for the people to vote upon it. But in that effort they failed so badly that today even their most faithful janissaries of yesterday are turning against them. The only friends they have left among the professional politicians are a few really sincere drys. But in the entire United States there are probably not a hundred professional politicians who are really sincere drys. In Maryland I can't think of one.

The reservations in the Republican plank look more formidable than they actually are. The most significant of them is that which declares for "retaining in the Federal government power to preserve the gains already made in dealing with the evils inherent in the liquor traffic." This is somewhat vague, but it apparently means no more than that the Federal government shall retain control over the importation of intoxicants, and shall have the right to protect dry States against floods of liquor from wet States. But these rights are surely not new. The Federal government, in fact, has had them since its birth, for they are plainly stated in Article 1, Section 8, of the Constitution.

Any attempt to extend them, say by providing that Congress shall have a right of veto over State liquor legislation, will be sure to set up a dreadful uproar, and the chances are that it will come to nothing. For behind the general demand that Prohibition be taken out of the Constitution is an even more resolute demand that the Federal government cease concerning itself with business which belongs properly to the States. This demand is certain to be voiced in the Democratic platform, and the Democratic candidate, whoever he is, is sure to whoop it up on the stump. Moreover, even the Republicans have heard and heeded it, and in the very plank we are discussing they promise to "allow the States to deal with the problem [of liquor] as their citizens may determine."

This, of course, is precisely what the Prohibitionists do *not* want. During the past year or two they have been ranting against States' rights almost as violently as they have been ranting against the saloon. The matter was discussed at every meeting of the dry shock-troops who lately toured the country, and their leader, the Rev. Daniel A. Poling, D. D., denounced the States' rights doctrine as treason every time he opened his mouth. But now, with Prohibition in collapse, the ancient rights of the States revive. Thus there is not much danger that the Federal government, when it divests itself of the Eighteenth Amendment at last, will attempt another and even more vexatious foray upon the States.

The question remains whether resubmission and repeal of the amendment can be expected within a reasonable time. It is not easy to answer. A good many wets, I suppose, assume that it is all over but the shouting, but that is by no means true. It would take a lot of hard sweating to get a resubmission resolution through the present House of Representatives, and even harder sweating to get it through the Senate. A two-thirds vote in each House would be necessary, and neither, so far, has shown so much as a bare majority against Prohibition.

To be sure, every politician in Washington now knows that Prohibition is done for, and so a great many of them may be expected to be converted to resubmission, and even to repeal within the next few weeks. Not a few have jumped already, and large numbers are known to be hesitating painfully. But the fact that they hesitate at all is proof enough that there may be several more slips between the cup and the lip, and in consequence an irksome delay. What worries these patriotic men is a keen realization, born of long experience, of the immense difference between what the people in general say they want, and how the morons in their concrete districts may be expected to vote. On more than one occasion in the past they have seen those morons beaten into line by the wizards of the Anti-Saloon League, and so they are going to be careful until they are dead certain that it can't happen again.

My belief is that, in many a congressional district, it *may* happen again, though perhaps only once more. The drys are still organized, they still have all the Methodist and Baptist pastors in their pen, and though they are broke nearly everywhere they are still able to holler. Thus I suspect that they'll be able to hold enough members in line to prevent the passage of the resubmission resolution by this Congress, and I even incline to believe that they may succeed again in the next Congress. The wets, remember, must summon up a two-thirds vote in each House. In the lower House they may do it by the time the next Congress comes in, but in the Senate it will be much more difficult, for only one-third of the present Senators go out in March, and those who will remain include most of the really honest drys.

Those honest drys—Smoot, Capper and company—deserve some respect, for their integrity if not for their sense. The real scoundrels are the turncoats who now flock to the wet side, deserting their allies and benefactors of many years. They are, even when they vote right, a knavish and disgusting gang of men, and I only hope that, when the chance offers, every self-respecting wet will help to retire them to private life. They have, for twelve years past, violated every decency by voting dry, and now they are ready to prove once more that they are prostitutes by voting for resubmission.

—X—

INTERLUDE: THE BISHOP STILL HOPES

[From the Sunday Sun, June 26, 1932] [1]

<hr />

Chicago, June 25

BISHOP JAMES CANNON, JR., the indomitable Peter the Hermit of the drys, has a phrase to describe the present unhappy state of Prohibition. It is, he told me this afternoon, "in the trough."

He admits freely that the dry evangel has got some hard blows of late, and he believes that it will probably get some even harder ones in the near future, but he is sure that it will survive, and even that it will enjoy a grand and glorious renaissance. The defection of so many hitherto

[1] This interview was written on Saturday evening, June 25. Inasmuch as there was no issue of the *Evening Sun* the next day it was turned over to the *Sunday Sun*.

dry statesmen, both Republican and Democratic, has neither surprised nor depressed him. He watches them leap, in fact, with the somewhat languid interest of a man who has been long aware that dogs will be dogs.

"Most of them," he told me, "were wet all the while. I knew it and so did everyone else who has any practical acquaintance with politicians. They voted dry so long as they believed that the majority of their constituents were dry, but in the face of the current wet uproar they are going over to the enemy.

"Unfortunately, it is too late in most cases for us to do anything about it. They have been nominated, and in many cases they are opposed by candidates who are also wet—in some cases, in fact, by candidates who have been wet all the while. If there had been time, we'd have opposed the nomination of a good many of them, and beaten them, but now it is too late. Thus we'll probably see some losses at the November election. But not as many, I think, as the wets expect."

"Do you think the wets will make enough gains to get a resubmission resolution through the next Congress?"

"I doubt it seriously. No matter how heavily the wet tide runs we'll be able to salvage at least forty per cent. of the members of the House, and probably more of the Senate. So the wets will be stuck. They may roll up a majority, but they will fall short of two-thirds, and so long as they fall short, Prohibition will be safe."

"But what of the present Congress? Suppose a lot more of your weakening drys go over to the opposition, and the wets get a two-thirds majority by December?"

"They can't do it," replied the bishop. "Their best chance will be, not in this Congress, but in the next one. But even in the next Congress they will fail to bag two-thirds of the members. In the Congress following, it will be our turn. We'll come back by then, and make plenty of gains. And so Prohibition will be safe for a long time to come."

I asked the bishop if he thought he could hold his own people in line—not the politicians but the rank and file of drys.

"I have no doubt of it," he replied. "I am, of course, too much of a realist to deny that some of them have been shaken. But shaken is really not the right word. I prefer to use amazed. They have been amazed by the apparent swing against Prohibition, and especially by the defection of John D. Rockefeller, Jr. The newspapers have made much of it, and every dry has heard of it. But as time passes they will also hear of the answers made to Mr. Rockefeller by Jane Addams, Commander Evangeline Booth of the Salvation Army, and other such drys, and then they will begin to think, and the more they think the more they will put up their backs."

"But don't you think they are going overboard almost as fast as the politicians? And that many of them are going overboard to stay?"

"Not at all. I was down in Tennessee last week at a big meeting of Southern teachers. They are all still as dry as ever. They crowded about me to tell me that they would stick. And our preachers, and those of the Baptists are still to be depended on. Do you hear of any of them coming out for repeal? Hardly. Well, they will begin preaching against it at full pressure in a little while, and they will keep on preaching against it until the present alarm is over.

"Our people have been caught rather unawares. They paid little attention to the campaign against Prohibition, for they knew that they couldn't be shaken themselves, and they assumed that no one else could be shaken. But now they are on notice that they must fight and soon they will be fighting as in the past. As I have said, I incline to believe that we may have something of a set-back in November, but if so it will be the last. After that, Prohibition will pull out of the trough, and go on to new and more durable victories."

His Grace told me that the Republican straddle on Prohibition was satisfactory to him, but I must add that he did not say it with anything reasonably described as enthusiasm.

"The chief virtue of it," he said, "is that it leaves every candidate for office free to take any line he pleases. He may come out wet and remain a good Republican, or he may come out dry. This is certainly better than if the convention had gone for repeal, and bound every candidate the same way."

Here I reminded him discreetly that his satisfaction was hard to square with the position of his friends before the convention.

"Didn't they advocate," I asked, "a straight Law Enforcement platform, binding every candidate to oppose repeal?"

His Grace admitted that something of the sort was undoubtedly in the heads of many of them, but hinted that in politics half a loaf is a great deal better than no bread. He was disinclined to discuss the position of Lord Hoover in the matter, save to point out that the right hon. gentleman, by the terms of the plank, was still free to restate his opposition to repeal, first made in his message accompanying the Wickersham Report. I asked him what he thought Lord Hoover would actually do, but he refused to make any prophecy.

"I really know no more about it," he said, "than you do. People seem to think that I am completely in Mr. Hoover's confidence, but it is not so. The truth is that I can recall talking to him no more than three times since he became President. It was the same in Harding's time. I believe I saw him twice altogether. But they had me climbing through the White House cellar windows every night."

The bishop refused to discuss the subject further, saying that he had troubles enough as it was, but I gather from other dry leaders that they take credit for the provision in the platform leaving every candidate free to be wet or dry as he pleases. They believe it will buck up many a politician, especially in the South, who has been wobbling under the wet attack. All that is needed to keep such tremblers in line, they argue, is enough whoopla on the dry side. This they propose to supply through the evangelical pastors.

The saving proviso was not in the original platform, as the Hon. Ogden L. Mills brought it to Chicago. But the drys made prompt and urgent representations in a certain exalted quarter and orders for the change seem to have come from that same quarter. The drys naturally cherish the proviso, for it was the only bone thrown to them. If they had failed to get it into the platform they would be down and out. As it is, they can argue that a dry may still be a good Republican.

The bishop and his friends refused today to predict what would be in the Democratic platform, but they were plainly without much hope that it would be drier than the Republican platform. The most they apparently look for is a proviso substantially like the one granted to them by the Republicans. This would save the face of any Democratic candidate who chose to continue dry, or to linger on the fence, but, by the same token, it would take in any dry who turned wet.

The drys will not make any definite plans for the campaign until the Democratic candidate is chosen and some word is had from Lord Hoover. They realize that the Democrat is very likely to be wetter than Hoover, and so their eyes turn hopefully in the direction of the White House. If Hoover declares against repeal, or makes another straddle, they will call another Asheville conference and try to bust the solid South again. But if he shows any signs of increasing wetness they will be against him, for it is their policy to support frank enemies rather than false friends.

Bishop Cannon, though he is disinclined to make any forecasts, doesn't believe that the Democratic candidate, whoever he is, will have an easy time carrying the big States of the Northeast.

"Even Al Smith," he said, "couldn't do it, and Al had a kind of support that the next candidate won't have. I dislike dragging in the religious question, and I had nothing to do with putting it into the last campaign, but everyone must be aware that there is a Catholic vote as well as a Protestant vote. Smith got it in 1928, but the candidate this year will be a Protestant, and so he can't count on it."

The bishop was booed at this afternoon's session of the platform committee, but he did not appear to resent it. He will linger in Chicago until the Democratic show is over, if it lasts all Summer. When it shuts down at last he will go to whatever conference is called by the drys, and then plunge into the campaign. He told me that he was fit and eager for action, and he looked it. He believes that the next few years will see the most violent battle over Prohibition that has ever been staged, and he is ready to leap into it with loud roars.

THE DEMOCRATS COME
TO TOWN

[From the Baltimore Evening Sun, June 27, 1932]

Chicago, June 27

IN THE hall but lately vacated by the Republicans
and still smelling strongly of the Hoover Pros-
perity, the Democrats met this afternoon to carry
out their quadrennial suicide pact. Theoretically,
they began the grim business at high noon, but
actually they gave themselves three-quarters of
an hour's grace. At 12.47 precisely Chairman
John J. Raskob banged his gavel and introduced
Commander Evangeline Booth of the Salvation
Army, who folded her hands, shut her eyes, and
discharged a long and murky prayer into the
microphone. The poor delegates had to stand

up all the while she harried Heaven, and most of
them were shuffling painfully before she finished.
There followed an Armenian lady singing "The
Star-Spangled Banner," and even the newspaper
reporters had to stand. The singer disclosed a
powerful mezzo-soprano, and did two stanzas of
the anthem with great *éclat*. Unfortunately, the
accompaniment of the band got out of step with
her, and so the music was turned into polyphony,
to the amazement of many and the joy of none.

There followed the usual speeches by local
worthies, including the mayor of Chicago. At 1.15
the unfortunate Raskob resumed his legs for his
last appearance as a statesman on this earth. It has
cost him fully a million dollars to be chairman
of the Democratic National Committee, but now
he must retire, and the money would have been
better invested if he had put it into Kreuger &
Toll. Raskob made a very plausible speech, but
it got only formal attention, and toward the end
of it there was a great deal of noise in the hall.
Dying politicians get the short shrift of steers in
the stockyards. Even when he denounced Prohibition, and bawled out the Republicans for their
straddle of two weeks ago, the applause he raised

was very faint. At 1.26 he disappeared into the shadows, and at 1.27 he was forgotten.

The tragedy of the convention is the collapse of Al Smith. Four years ago, even in the face of crushing defeat, he stood forth as the dominant personage of his party, but when he leaves Chicago this time it will be to join such ghosts as John W. Davis, of Wall Street, W. Va., and the Mr. Cox who ran so evanescently in 1920, and whose front name I now forget. As these lines are written it is the gossip that he still plans to take the floor and deliver a powerful tirade against Roosevelt, but if he does so he will be very badly advised. For the more powerful his tirade the more good it will do to Roosevelt and the more damage to Al Smith. Roosevelt himself, of course, is anything but popular, either in the convention or outside. I can recall no candidate of like importance who ever had so few fanatics whooping for him. His followers here are as silent as if they were up to something unpalatable to the police. The small band of Garner men (and ex-Garner men) from Texas is making at least ten times as much noise. If there are any Roosevelt buttons on tap I have not seen them, and Roosevelt portraits are so scarce that Ritchie portraits outnumber them at least ten to one. The whole Roosevelt fight is being carried on in a curiously stealthy and *pianissimo* manner.

The reason is plain enough. It is that at least a majority of the Roosevelt men are really not for Roosevelt at all, but simply against Al Smith. They want to get rid of Al, once and for all time, some of them because they believe more or less rationally that he has become a liability to the party, but most of them, I suspect, because they are still Ku Kluxers at heart. Al represents something that they can't understand, and hence view with suspicion. He is, by their peculiar standards, a foreigner, an idolator and a generally dubious character. In 1928 he led some of them down to defeat and disaster and forced the rest into a party treason that they are still ashamed of. So they are against him—and any stick is good enough to beat a dog with.

The special merit of Roosevelt in their eyes, and perhaps his only real merit, is that Al seems to hate him. Thus the more Al rants against him the more firmly those who favor him will stick to him. This is half of the melancholy story. The other half is that the anti-Roosevelt factions have been unable to concentrate upon a candidate, and thus find themselves in the unhappy position of the bright lads who tried to stop old Charlie Curtis at the recent Republican convention. Very few of the delegates at that convention were actually in favor of Charlie, but they could not find anyone to beat him with, and so he laughed at them and got his renomination without a struggle.

The only anti-Roosevelt group that is really determined to fight Roosevelt to the death is the Smith group, and even it is near disintegration. The rest are all ready to trade with the ostensible enemy, and some of them have already made scarcely disguised overtures. This leaves poor Al hanging out on a branch, and unless a miracle happens he will presently hear an alarming crackling near the trunk of the tree. His job was to organize the Roosevelt opposition, and at that he has failed completely. It was holding together far better, indeed, a week ago than it is holding together today.

Al's failure has been due in part to the irreconcilable opposition of his old enemies, the Bible students, especially in the South, but it has also been due in part to the decay of his own technique. He was, in his day, one of the most adept politicians ever heard of in America. He had all of the professional skill of a Tammany leader of long experience, and in addition he had some tricks that were all his own, and not a few of them were tricks that did quite as much credit to his wisdom as to his mere cleverness. But the Al of today is no longer a politician of the first chop. His association with the rich has apparently wobbled him and changed him. He has become a golf player. In a championship match with the whole country looking on he has been outsmarted by a former padrone of prize-fighters. It is a sad spectacle.

Governor Ritchie and his friends are also out on a branch, but there are some soft mattresses under them, and not the broken bottles that menace poor Al. They have made no enemies anywhere, and in particular they have made none in the Roosevelt camp. They are still in opposition, but they have not failed to consider certain eventualities. They have been greatly aided in this policy of courtesy and conciliation by the fact that, as delegations to national conventions go, they are extremely high in tone. Not many delegations ever show so many genuinely distinguished men.

The contrast with the State's Republican delegation at the convention of two weeks ago is almost ludicrous. Maryland sent to the Republican gathering a gang of dismal jobholders, with a few third-rate Babbitts to perfume them. The delegation played an obscure and unedifying part in the convention. It was heard from, in fact, only when the time came to vote, and always it cast a united vote that might have been cast just as well by a machine. But the Maryland delegation to the present convention enjoys an importance far outrunning its modest numbers, and many of its members are conspicuous figures and are getting a lot of attention.

This is especially true of the two Johns Hopkins *Gelehrten,* Drs. Hugh H. Young and Dean Lewis. Dr. Lewis is an old Chicagoan and he seems to be very well remembered here. If the exigencies of statecraft left him the time he would be eating fifty or sixty dinners a day and attending from one to two hundred parties of a literary and scientific nature in the evening. As for Dr. Young, he is surrounded all day by his grateful alumni, many of whom say they owe their capacity to take part in the week's great historic ceremonies to his subtle cobbling.[1]

The booze supply seems to be ample, but prices continue to be high. The police have raided a few speakeasies, but enough remain open to take the edge off the hot weather. But the Marylanders, I suspect, will be glad to get back to the Free State, where the booticians are all masters of their art and do not expect to get rich in less than six months.

[1] It is scarcely necessary to explain, I hope, that Dr. Young is clinical professor of urology at the Johns Hopkins Medical School, and the originator of a famous operation for prostatitis. He has, in his day, relieved many an elderly Americano of serious impediments to a happy life, and among his patients have been large numbers of statesmen. They greeted him warmly at Chicago and promised to vote for his candidate, Governor Ritchie, but nearly all of them forgot to do so when the time came. Dr. Lewis is professor of surgery at the Johns Hopkins, chief surgeon of the Johns Hopkins Hospital, and president of the American Medical Association.

—XII—

PRELIMINARY POSTURES
AND GRIMACES

[From the Baltimore Evening Sun, June 28, 1932]

Chicago, June 28

THE SECOND day of the convention began with blood dripping from the moon, and every prospect of an old-time Democratic shambles, with no less than four gory bouts on the card, as follows:

1. There are bitter contests in three States, and at least two of them threaten to be taken to the floor. In one of these the celebrated Louisiana Kingfish, Huey Long, is a central figure. He took the floor in defense of his batch of delegates this afternoon, and made a speech that got him a cheer and won him his fight.

2. There will be a grand and gaudy battle over the permanent chairmanship, with each side convinced up to the last minute that it can win, and under that battle will rage the implacable combat between Roosevelt

and Al Smith, which has long since passed the stage of asking or giving quarter.

3. Then will come the platform fight. Even so late as yesterday it promised to be mild and polite, with no real contest between the two factions of wets, but now they are both steaming up, and will probably fall upon one another in a furious and merciless manner, even though they agree on all essentials.

4. There will follow the nominations themselves. Two days ago the Roosevelt men were confident that they had it all their own way, but now they begin to be harassed by doubts, and the opposition is eagerly pressing home every advantage that is in those doubts. No one talks of quick action any more. It promises to be a long, tedious and exhausting struggle on grunt-and-growl principles.

Ordinarily, a contest before the credentials committee has little repercussion on the floor. The committee solves the problem as best it can and the convention follows its lead, with maybe half an hour or so of formal oratory. But this time there was at least one contest that stirred the convention, and that was the one between Huey Long and his enemies in Louisiana. All of the Southerners were actively interested in it. They saw in it a combat between an elder and more decorous South and the new and blatant South that Huey represents. They didn't want to see Huey win against the courtly old ex-Governor Saunders, but he is a very tough baby and they weren't able to help it.

The contest over the permanent chairmanship is full of bellicose possibilities. In general it may be said that the Roosevelt side is dominant in the committee, where each State and territory, however small, has one vote, but very uncertain of its strength before the convention, where the vote is by delegates, and a State with a lot of them can outvote one with only a few. Here the unit rule adds to the complications of the situation. There will not only be the grand bout between the two main factions, but also a series of smaller but no less bitter bouts in the delegations.

Up to noon it seemed likely that there would also be a venomous fight over the Roosevelt effort to abrogate the two-thirds rule and to postpone consideration of the platform until after the nominations. First, the Roosevelt people tried to get rid of the two-thirds rule altogether, and then they proposed to abandon it after eight ballots. But today, James A. Farley, the Roosevelt manager, suddenly threw up the sponge, evidently on orders received from Mr. Roosevelt himself, and so there will be no fight on the floor. This surrender has naturally cheered the anti-Roosevelt forces very greatly, and especially the Ritchie men.

Farley offered in the end to give up his fight to abrogate the two-thirds rule if the allies would agree to postpone consideration of the platform until after the nominations. But the allies refused to do business on that basis, and so Farley had to yield everything. The only consolation he got was a promise to recommend the abrogation of the two-thirds rule hereafter. But that is too vague to be worth much, and moreover it won't do him any good in this convention.

The abandonment of the scheme to postpone the platform is also a striking victory for the opposition. The Roosevelt people wanted to get the nomination over with before the platform came up, on the ground that the longer they had to wait the harder it would be to hold their votes together. They also feared that the platform fight might develop some serious animosities, and so further split their delegations. But now they are resigned to taking the full dose, and the spectators will see only four great combats instead of five or six. The four, however, promise to be very juicy.

After a session in the quarters of Mayor Howard W. Jackson of Baltimore, lasting the better part of the night, the really wet wets, led by Senator David I. Walsh of Massachusetts and Major E. Brooke Lee of Maryland, emerged this morning with the following plank against Prohibition:

> We favor the repeal of the Eighteenth Amendment.
>
> We demand that the Congress immediately propose such repeal to truly representative conventions in the States.
>
> We urge that the Democratic party coöperate in the enactment of such measures by the several States as will actually promote temperance, effectively prevent the return of the saloon, and bring the liquor traffic into the open, under complete supervision and control by the States.
>
> We demand that the Federal government effectively exercise its power to protect States against importation of intoxicating liquors in violation of their laws.
>
> Pending repeal, we favor immediate modification of the Volstead Act to legalize the manufacture and sale of beer and other beverages of such alcoholic content as is permissible under the Constitution, and to provide therefrom a proper and needed revenue.

In the course of the long debate, this plank underwent several changes. In its first form there was no mention of the revenue from beer and light wines, and the section reserving the Federal government the right to prevent the shipment of liquor into dry States was rather more sweeping. According to Mayor Jackson, the plank has been signed by the representatives of twenty-three States and more are expected to sign before the day is out.

Just after the convention met the extreme wets of the resolutions committee inserted another tooth in their plank. It consists of the words "called to act solely on that proposal," and it follows the words "truly representative conventions in the States" in Section 2. The wets say they are getting more signatures every hour and that they will have enough when the time comes to put over their plank with a whoop.

The most important section of the plank is the one which advocates an immediate repeal of the Volstead Act. This goes much further than the Republican plank. It is sure to arouse the drys to a bitter, last-ditch fight, and they may have until the end of the week to bring up their artillery. At the most, the matter will go to the floor and provoke a heated debate, with all of the ill humors hanging over from the nomination to add to its rancors.

Altogether, the convention promises to be full of alarms and surprises, bludgeonings and mayhems. When the delegates got to town on Sunday all the prospects seemed to run the other way. Roosevelt, it appeared, would be jammed through with scarcely a yell from anyone save Al Smith. But now it is plain that he will have to fight ferociously every inch of the way, and his maneuvers so far show that his victory is by no means certain. Thus the convention lines up for an old-time Democratic battle royal. The brethren sniff the scent of battle. The air will be full of hair and ears within twenty-four hours.

INTERLUDE: A DRY VIEWS THE CARNAGE

[From the Baltimore Evening Sun, June 28, 1932]

Chicago, June 28

COL. PATRICK H. CALLAHAN, of Louisville, Ky., the last survivor of the *bloc* of Irish Catholic Prohibitionists, which at its peak consists of no less than eight or nine members, lay and clerical, and some say even ten, has come to town to view the remains of the holy cause. He realizes that bringing it back to life would be a miracle far beyond human power, even if the whole Irish nation pitched in to help, but he hopes that he will yet be able to induce the platform committee to lay a wreath of lilies on the casket. He has a plank to that end, and showed it to me confidentially, but refused to let it be published.

"Call it throwing us a bone," he said, "if you please, but certainly we deserve something. The Methodist and Baptist drys are going to support Hoover. Put that down, and you won't go wrong. The way is open for him to be nice to them. But what are we Catholic Democratic drys going to do? I hope the party gives us something. We don't ask for much, but we ought to have something."

I observed that the colonel seemed to believe that Prohibition had struck a snag. He threw up his hands and said: "Don't mention it!" and then went on with the sad story as he sees it.

"They are jumping out of every window," he said. "There goes Carter Glass. There goes Morris Sheppard. I wonder how many we have left. Maybe Smoot, the Mormon, and certainly Cordell Hull.[1] But who else? I leave you to figure it out for yourself.

"What busted us? Simply bad leadership. Simply that gang of professionals. Every one of them was trying to set up shop on his own. You know how it is in business. You train up a drummer

[1] Three days later Senator Hull was before the convention defending the minority (once the majority) plank, which provided for resubmission? See No. XVI.

and as soon as he gets good he wants to go into business for himself. Well, the professional Prohibitionists are pretty much the same. One of them organized the West in his own name. And another gobbled Pennsylvania, a big State, and in those days full of money. And so it went, until the country was peppered with dry organizations, many of them private snaps.

"They could never agree about anything. When Mr. Hoover appointed the Wickersham Commission and it began to take testimony I proposed that all the dry forces tackle it as a unit and in writing, to save time and breath. But pretty soon this or that professional was going after this or that member on his own hook, and in the end the commission got such an overdose that it began to turn wet. I believe its report was a body blow to Prohibition. We have never been the same since."

The colonel said that he began to be in favor of making terms with the wets so long ago as September, 1930. At that time he attended a conference in New York which included Frank Gannett, the publisher of a string of dry newspapers; Fred B. Smith, head of the Committee of One Thousand, an organization of rich drys; Col. Raymond

A DRY VIEWS THE CARNAGE

Robbins, the Rev. Daniel A. Poling, and Willis J. Abbott, editor of the *Christian Science Monitor*.

Franklin A. Fort, the dry New Jersey Representative, still had six months to serve in the House and the conference decided to ask him to submit a resubmission resolution and get the agony over. Deets Pickett and the Rev. Dr. Clarence True Wilson approved this decision, but F. Scott McBride, the Rev. A. D. Barton, boss of the Baptist drys, and other leaders opposed it and so it came to nothing.

"After that," said the colonel, "it was every man for himself. The dry outfit was divided and full of dissension. What those fellows lack is the capacity to give and take. They have no sense of humor. The whole Prohibition movement would have been much better off if there had been more Irish in it. You can't do much with Puritans. They are too sure about everything."

The colonel believes that if Roosevelt is nominated he will be beaten.

"The Catholic vote in all the big cities," he said, "will be cast against him. They will never forgive him for stealing the nomination from Al Smith. True enough, Al would have been beaten, too, and perhaps even worse, but you will never convince them of that. All of the Catholic papers are denouncing Roosevelt today. It only proves once more what I have always argued: that priests are the dumbest politicians ever heard of."

"But what," I asked, "if Al decides to bury the hatchet, and takes to the stump for Roosevelt?"

"He probably won't do it," replied the colonel, "but even if he does it won't do any good. The only way to save the Catholic vote is to get rid of Roosevelt altogether. But that begins to look impossible. Myself, I am for Melvin A. Traylor. He could carry all of the big cities of the North. As for the South, let it take care of itself. It will hardly follow the professional drys again. Any Democrat can carry it. But Traylor seems to be out of the race and Roosevelt looks the winner. Let them nominate him and see what happens. He will be beaten worse than Al. He won't carry a single big State."

The colonel believes that a resubmission resolution will get through both houses of Congress at the December session. He is not impressed by the fact that the drys maintained their majority on every recent test.

A DRY VIEWS THE CARNAGE

"The boys," he said, "are falling away by battalions and regiments. They all want to get on the wet bandwagon. Look at that fellow Alben W. Barkley, of my own State of Kentucky. I remember the time when he was actually working for the Anti-Saloon League. He did it for a percentage of the receipts. And yet I sat in the convention hall yesterday afternoon and heard him bellow for resubmission and repeal. That's the way it is going. I trust a few of them, but not many. Cordell Hull will stick, I am sure. Nothing can scare Hull. But the rest of them are jumping."

The colonel believes, however, that it will be possible to stop the resubmission resolution when it comes to the States. He insists that multitudes of the plain people are still dry, and will show it when the time comes to vote for members of the State conventions. The politicians, he admits, are running amuck, but the plain people still stand fast. His reasons for so believing unfortunately are not quite clear, and so I do not venture to state them. In the main they seem to revolve around a doubt about the *Literary Digest* poll. He believes that most of the real drys held aloof from it.

I asked him if he thought that Prohibition,

supposing that it is saved as he hopes, will eve[r] be enforced. He replied that a really strong ma[n] might enforce it, and mentioned William G. Mc Adoo. But at once he hedged on McAdoo an[d] turned to Mussolini.

"I suppose," he said, "that it would take [a] Mussolini. We don't seem to have one at the mo ment, but maybe we'll get one later on. However, even a Mussolini could hardly make a clean sweep of it. The country club people will prob ably go on boozing until the end of time. The best Prohibition can hope to accomplish is to save the poor man. It saves him by making drink too ex pensive for him."

I asked the colonel what he thought would follow Prohibition, supposing the Eighteenth Amendment repealed.

"That," he said, somewhat gloomily, "is a hell of a question. Only God knows what the answer is."

—XIV—

INTERLUDE: HOME TOWN STUFF

[From the Baltimore Evening Sun, June 28, 1932]

Chicago, June 28

GOVERNOR RITCHIE is being bombarded today by telegrams from radio fans who heard his broadcast on Prohibition last night. They are coming in from half the States of the Union, including Vermont, Nebraska and California. All of them seem to be from wets.

The Governor ran into unexpected luck last night. The original plan was that he should share his time with William G. McAdoo, who still leans somewhat toward the dry side, but McAdoo failed to show up and so Ritchie had it all to himself. He gave the fans a large dose of wet doctrine.

MAKING A PRESIDENT

The Maryland delegation is following a cautious programme. It is hard at work operating on the anti-Roosevelt delegates and at the same time trying to avoid outraging the Roosevelt men. The business of tackling the Southerners has been largely in the hands of Dr. Hugh H. Young, who speaks the Confederate dialect fluently and has been a lifelong admirer of the late Gen. Robert E. Lee. Dr. Young put in most of the morning with the Alabama delegation, and he is now working his way across the Cotton Belt to North Carolina.

The fight for a really wet plank on Prohibition has been carried on largely by E. Brooke Lee and Mayor Howard W. Jackson. Mr. Lee is the Maryland member of the resolutions committee and Mr. Jackson has been taken into the inner circle of uncompromising wets. The Governor himself spent the morning seeing visitors in his quarters.

Everywhere he goes he is accompanied by Patrolman Matt Henderson, of the Chicago police force, in full uniform. There is no fear that anyone contemplates putting him on the spot, but like all the other conspicuous figures of the convention he is unpleasantly beset by wild-eyed propagandists and other nuisances. Patrolman Henderson is armed with clubs, gas bombs and firearms, and can thus take care of them. But so far the mere sight of his uniform has sufficed to cool them off.

XV

TWO GANGS OF WETS

[From the Baltimore Evening Sun, June 29, 1932]

———————————————

Chicago, June 29

TODAY, ALL the spotlights are concentrated upon
the deathbed of Prohibition. It is dying a much
quieter death than anyone seems to have expected.
In fact, it has been virtually unconscious since the
Republican convention of two weeks ago. Nor are
the chief mourners doing any noticeable weeping.
They are all, or nearly all, still in town—Bishop
Cannon, Dr. Ernest H. Cherrington, Dr. F. Scott
McBride and the rest—but nothing has been heard
from them for two days, and there was no sign of
them when the resolutions committee met to sign
the death certificate this morning.

TWO GANGS OF WETS

Major E. Brooke Lee, the Maryland member, went into the committee meeting expecting to see his ultra-wet plank made the majority plank. Up to last night the members from twenty-three States and territories had signed it, and this morning several more fell into the procession. Only twenty-eight names are needed to displace the official plank, drawn up by A. Mitchell Palmer. But even if the committee rejects the Lee plank, Mr. Lee looks for it to prevail on the floor, for among the States that favor it are most of the larger ones, and on the floor their strength counts in votes, whereas in committee each has but one vote.

The committee will report to the convention as soon as it can agree, probably by the middle of the afternoon. The difference between the two planks is really not serious. Both, to the dry eye, look enormously wet. Both provide for an early referendum, both submit the question of repeal to State conventions elected for the purpose, and both promise to protect dry States against inundations from the wet States. But the Lee plank also declares for the immediate amendment of the Volstead Act, to let in light wines and beer, and it is this difference that has caused the only serious debate in the committee.

In brief, the whole combat is between two gangs of wets, one of them a shade wetter than the other. But even the drier gang, in the sight of the Prohibitionists, is dripping wet. Thus, the Democrats finish the butchery started by the Republicans. Prohibition is left without a single salient friend in either party. Four years ago both conventions were full of its advocates, and the chief professional Prohibitionists were heard with a degree of deference verging upon reverence. But now they are outsiders, and nobody seems to know where they are, what they are doing, or what they have to say. Some of them have thrown up the sponge, and the rest are in a very low state of mind.

Major Henry H. Curran, head of the Association Opposed to the Prohibition Amendment, believes that the wet women, whether fashionable or otherwise, have had a great deal to do with the sudden and melodramatic collapse of Prohibition.

"What made them extraordinarily effective," he said today, "is the fact that they were able to get at the concrete politician. There was no way for him to throw them off. He simply had to stand and listen, and the more he listened the more it became plain to him that he was up against a really irresistible uprising. So he began to hunt for cover, and when he saw other politicians in both parties doing the same thing the great retreat began. The fight offered the women their first chance to show that they could think for themselves in politics and, what is more, the first chance to prove that they had a very real power. The drys had been depicting all women as natural Prohibitionists, which was just as offensive to intelligent women as it would have been to intelligent men. So they leaped at the opportunity to give the dry evangelists a beating, and they certainly did the job in a hearty and spectacular manner."

Major Curran is against any excessive haste in getting a repeal resolution through Congress. He believes that waiting a bit will consolidate the wet position and so make a clean and decisive victory all the more certain. The surviving drys, he believes, will try to compromise, and he is against any compromise.

"We must get rid of Prohibition," he said, "once and forever. It must be buried so deep that even the craziest fanatic will abandon all hope of exhuming it. The country wants to destroy it and forget it. Among fair and sensible men it has no more friends."

Major Curran believes that getting a repeal resolution through Congress will be easy, and that getting it through the State conventions will be even easier.

"By the time we come to that," he said, "there will be no more dry States. It would even be safe to trust the business to the State Legislatures. Prohibition is in complete collapse. There is nothing left for us save the mopping up."

XVI

THE WET WETS TRIUMPH

[From the Baltimore Evening Sun, June 30, 1932]

Chicago, June 30

Since one o'clock this morning Prohibition has been a fugitive in the remote quagmires of the Bible Belt. The chase began thirteen hours earlier, when the resolutions committee of the convention retired to the voluptuous splendors of the Rose Room at the Congress Hotel. For four hours nothing came out of the apartment save the moaning of converts in mighty travail. Then the Hon. Michael L. Igoe, a round-faced Chicago politician, burst forth with the news that the wet wets of the committee had beaten the damp wets by a vote of 35 to 17. There ensued a hiatus, while the quarry panted and the bloodhounds bayed. At seven in the evening the chase was resumed in the stadium, and four hours later Prohibition went out of the window to the stately tune of $934\frac{3}{4}$ to $213\frac{1}{4}$, or more than four to one. So the flight to the fastnesses of Zion began.

But even down there, where Genesis has the police behind it and an unbaptized man is as rare as a metaphysician, the fugitive is yet harried and oppressed. Only two States, Georgia and Mississippi, showed a solid dry front on the poll, and in Georgia there were plenty of wets lurking behind the unit rule. All the other great Commonwealths of the late Confederacy cast votes for the immediate repeal of the Eighteenth Amendment and the Volstead Act, led by Texas with its solid 46, and South Carolina with its solid 18. Even Tennessee, the Baptist Holy Land, went 18 dripping wet to 6 not so wet. Taking all the Confederate States together, with Kentucky thrown in, they cast 165 votes for the forthright and uncompromising plank of the rebellious majority, and only 123 for the pussyfooting plank of the docile minority. In the Middle West the carnage was even more appalling. Kansas voted

12 to 8 for the minority straddle, but Iowa went the whole hog with loud hallelujahs, and so did North Dakota, and so did Indiana and Illinois. Even Ohio, the citadel of the Anti-Saloon League, went over to the enemy by 49 to 2, and Nebraska, the old home of William Jennings Bryan, voted nearly two to one for rum and rebellion.

It was a gorgeous affair while it lasted, and the consolations for the poor drys were precious few and not very stimulating. They held Mississippi, the Worst American State,[1] and they held Oklahoma, and the better part of Arkansas, Alabama and North Carolina, but these States are all wabbling, and not even the most optimistic friend of the late holy cause expects them to hold out much longer.

The fight in the resolutions committee was full of dramatic surprises, but by the time it was transferred to the floor of the convention the end was plainly in sight, and so it narrowly escaped becoming a bore. When the really wet wets, led by Senator David I. Walsh of Massachusetts and Major E. Brooke Lee of Maryland went into the committee room they had but twenty-three States

[1] See the *American Mercury* for September, October and November, 1931.

pledged to their side, and they needed twenty-eight. Major Lee professed to be sure that he could snare them, but his confidence was anything but visible on his face. A long, long wait followed, with a gang of reporters buzzing around the keyhole. Nothing came out of it, and all of the statesmen who emerged at intervals turned out to be deaf and dumb. The hotel was as hot as a boiler room, and every time the door opened the eminent men within could be seen mopping their bald heads.

Suddenly, at three o'clock, the Hon. Mr. Igoe popped out.

"The vote," he bawled, "is 35 to 18."

"For what?" demanded the reporters.

"Against the majority plank."

"Do you mean that the wet wets have substituted the Walsh plank?"

"Not yet," replied the Hon. Mr. Igoe. "One thing at a time. First we had to reject the majority plank. Now we'll take up"—

But at that precise moment another statesman burst out with the news that it was done—that the Walsh plank had been substituted by a vote of 35 to 17. What became of the odd vote was never made plain.

The session of the convention, meanwhile, had been postponed from noon to one o'clock, and then to three, and then to seven. Everyone looked for the resolutions committee to wrestle with the Prohibition plank all afternoon, and maybe far into the night. But when the plank was reached, after a long and innocuous debate over the tariff, war debts and free silver, the fight was over in ten minutes. For the wet wets, reinforced by their twelve converts, demanded a showdown instantly, and it proved that they had an overwhelming majority. Moreover, it proved that the majority on the floor would be very much larger, for in committee each State had only one vote, whereas on the floor it would cast a vote for every one of the delegates, and the big States were all on the wet-wet side.

Thus combat on the floor was really only a sham battle, though it lasted more than three hours. When former Senator Gilbert M. Hitchcock of Nebraska got on his legs to read the report of the committee—which is to say, to read the platform—there was such turmoil in the hall that Chairman Thomas J. Walsh had to bang for

order over and over again. But when Mr. Hitchcock approached the Prohibition plank there was
a sudden hush, and the instant the first sentence
of it was out of his mouth the roof was shaken
by a stupendous cheer. At once the delegations
began parading, led by South Carolina from the
traitorous Bible Belt and Iowa from the recreant
open spaces of the Middle West. Mississippi
held out, and so did Virginia, Washington, Oklahoma, Delaware, North Carolina and Alabama,
but there was almost as much politeness in this
as fidelity, for three hours later the seven of them
were to yield $38\frac{1}{2}$ wet-wet votes.

The first rhetorician put up to speak for the
minority report, which had been the majority report until the catastrophe in the Rose Room, was
the Hon. Cordell Hull of Tennessee. The Hon.
Mr. Hull is a Prohibitionist of long service and
heroic deeds, and only three days ago Col.
Patrick H. Callahan, the lone Catholic dry, was
telling me that he would be the last stalwart to
surrender to the Rum Demon. And yet here he
was pleading for resubmission of the Eighteenth
Amendment! Not a word did he utter in favor of
Prohibition. All he had to say was that it would

be better to put it on trial in a decorous and judicial manner, and not butcher it out of hand. The crowd yelled him down.

"You are proposing to repeal Prohibition," he yelled, "after only a few hours' consideration."

"Twelve years," yelled some one in the gallery, and once more Chairman Walsh had to get out his bungstarter and clout for order. It came after awhile and the long debate proceeded. All sorts of orators were put up. Some of them spoke for as little as two minutes. Most of them were local dignitaries, eager only to reach the radio audience back home. They offered little in the way of argument and nothing in the way of eloquence. Four-fifths of them seemed to be hotly in favor of the wet-wet plank, but sometimes it was difficult to make out which side a given speaker was on.

One such was a gentleman from Texas, whose name seemed to be Hughes. He was introduced as a defender of the minority plank and the crowd started to boo him, but at once he announced that Texas had decided unanimously to join the wet wets and so the boos began to be drowned in cheers. As he proceeded it appeared that he was actually arguing for the majority plank, which is to say, for light wines and beers immediately and the harder stuff on some near and blest tomorrow. Whether Chairman Walsh made a mistake in introducing him or he became converted to the wet wet doctrine while he was on his legs never appeared clearly. But the crowd decided that he was all right and when the gavel cut him short he was given a rousing hullabaloo for his pains.

The so-called debate went on in the brutal, clumsy, ribald manner that is almost as characteristic of a national convention as the June heat. Delegate after delegate, some male and some female, climbed up on the platform to heave another projectile at the vanishing shadows of Prohibition. They came not only from the traditionally wet and antinomian States but also from such former paradises of Christian Endeavor as Florida, Iowa and South Carolina. Their names were often unintelligible, and what they had to say was only half heard. But now and then a notable was recognized and got his round of huzzahs. Thus it was that the late Jouett Shouse of

THE WET WETS TRIUMPH

Kansas, leaping eagerly from his tomb, was given his chance to hymn his fellow-corpse, the Hon. John J. Raskob, and to say all over again that Prohibition is, was and of a right ought to be a great curse to humanity. Some of these snorters against it looked to me to be very recent converts. In fact, not a few of them appeared to be still packing Bibles on their hips, and more than one did his stuff in the ecstatic singsong of a retrieved hell-cat at a revival.

The debate was supposed to proceed in the orthodox manner, with each side using half the time, but it was soon apparent that the opponents of the wet-wet plank had very few word-heavers on their string, and that none of them was actually dry. The best was probably a gentleman from Idaho, who looked like a prosperous cattleman, and made a plea for the simple resubmission of the Eighteenth Amendment without any party commitment either one way or the other. He was heard more or less politely until he squared off and demanded "Is it fair to say that in order to qualify as a Democrat a man must be wet?" Shouts of "Yes! Yes!" went up from both the floor and the galleries and the services had to be halted to give the ultra-wets a chance a howl off some of their libido.

The great set piece of the debate was the speech of Al Smith. When he suddenly appeared on the platform, his face a brilliant scarlet and his collar wet and flapping about his neck, he got a tremendous reception and the overgrown pipe organ let loose with "East Side, West Side" in an almost terrifying manner, with every stop wide open and a ton or so of extra weight on the safety valve. Al did a very good job. He had at Lord Hoover with some excellent wisecracks, he made some amusing faces, and he got a huge and friendly laugh by pronouncing the word radio in his private manner, with two d's. He had sense enough to shut down before he wore out his welcome, and so he got another ear-splitting hand as he finished, with the organ booming again and the band helping.

Governor Ritchie had been told off to second Al's efforts, but a lot of obscure wet wets were panting to be heard by the folk back home, and he had to wait nearly two hours. He put in the time on the platform, mopping his neck, for the heat increased as the evening wore on, and by midnight it was that of Washington on a muggy August afternoon. In the end the Governor came near being robbed of his chance by a stout old fellow named W. C. Fitts, with a glittering bald head and bushy white eyebrows.

The Hon. Mr. Fitts turned out to be from Birmingham, Ala., and he arose to plead with the delegates to abate their wet fervor a trifle, so as to avoid putting the party on a series of red-hot spots in the surviving dry strongholds of the Bible Belt. He had a plausible case, and he urged it in a reasonable manner. Not a word in favor of Prohibition came out of him. He simply asked that the Southern delegates be spared the need of going home smelling too powerfully of the devil's brews. But the crowd was hot for the wet-test imaginable wetness, and pretty soon it began to boo him and to demand a vote. The old boy, however, stuck to the microphone, and whenever his syllogisms and exhortations were drowned out by the uproar Chairman Walsh went furiously to his rescue. He kept going, first and last, for at least twenty minutes and in the end he had his say. But he had got the galleries into such a lather that it began to look like suicide for Governor Ritchie to follow him.

Nevertheless, the Governor stepped into it, and at sight of him the crowd shed its impatience magically, and he got a rousing reception, with the organ booming "Maryland, My Maryland" and "Dixie." He had prepared a speech running to a column in the *Evening Sun,* and it had been sent out to the four corners of the Republic by the press associations, but he wisely abandoned it and gave them something shorter and snappier. It made an excellent success, and when he sat down there was another roar, and the organ took another herculean hack at "Maryland, My Maryland."

When the voting began at midnight it was apparent at once that the extreme wets had it all their own way, and that the resubmission plank of the minority, though it went much further than the Republican straddle, was too mild to poll any considerable vote. When Alabama split and Arizona cast its six votes for the majority plank the whole audience, delegates and visitors alike, began to cheer, and thereafter the voting was carried on in the traditional Democratic manner, to the tune of howls, bellowings and charges of fraud. Three delegations demanded polls and caused long delays, and there were numerous hot exchanges between the chair and the floor. But the wet vote rolled up steadily, and by the time Kansas was reached it was running two to one. When Massachusetts threw in thirty-six wet votes it rose to three to one, and at the end it was better than four to one.

Despite the slow tempo, the polling was full of dramatic episodes. Just as Iowa, for long a happy hunting ground of the Anti-Saloon League, went dripping wet with all its delegates on their legs, yelling and waving their hats, a courier entered the press stand with the news that Senator George W. Norris, of Nebraska, one of the last of the honest drys in Washington, had come out for resubmission and confessed that Prohibition was a cooked goose. Ten minutes later the Nebraska Democrats cast nine votes for the wet-wet plank and only five for the damp one, with one delegate absent and another too alarmed and upset to vote.

The sweep was really colossal. No comfort whatever was left for the drys. Two weeks ago the Republican convention threw them some

bones, but the Democrats characteristically refused to do so. The plank adopted is the wettest
ever proposed by even the most fanatical wet—
in fact, it goes beyond anything that was so much
as imagined a month ago, or even two weeks ago.
After the Republican convention the professional drys were full of hope that they would be
able to intimidate the Democrats into compromise and futility. But the Democrats simply refused to be intimidated. Instead, they fell upon
Prohibition with raucous howls, gave it a dreadful beating and then chased it back to the Bible
country whence it came.

The professional drys gave up the fight yesterday morning. They are astute fellows and they
saw, even before the wet leaders, which way the
thing was going. I tried to find Bishop Cannon
to hear his last words, but though he seemed to
be in Chicago no one could locate him. He and
his friends will now call another Asheville conference and prepare to arouse the Southern Bible
students for Hoover again. But it will be much
harder this time and they know it. In 1928 they
had a candidate who could help them, for the
legend of the Great Engineer was still in full

blast. But now they are strapped to a corpse and the once so amiable Yahweh of the club and the search-warrant has deserted them.

XVII

THE ALL-NIGHT SESSION

[From the Baltimore Evening Sun, July 1, 1932]

Chicago, July 1

THE PLAN of the Roosevelt managers to rush the convention and put over their candidate with a bang failed this morning, and after a turbulent all-night session and two roll-calls the anti-Roosevelt men fought off a motion to adjourn until this afternoon and the delegates proceeded to a third test of strength.

A few minutes before the first roll-call began, at 4 o'clock this morning, Arthur F. Mullen, of Nebraska, Farley's chief of staff, told me that Roosevelt would receive 675 votes on the first ballot and 763 on the second, and that the third would bring him the two-thirds needed for his nomination. But the first ballot actually brought him only 666¼ and the second only 677¾, and the third had not gone halfway down the roll of States before it was plainly evident that a hard fight was ahead of him, with his chances much slimmer than they seemed to be the time the voting began. In brief, the Roosevelt runaway was stopped.

The first two ballots were taken amid the utmost confusion and to the tune of loud and raucous challenges from unhappy minorities of various delegations. On the first ballot Minnesota demanded to be polled, with the result that its 24 votes under the unit rule went to Roosevelt. New York, which was also polled, split unequally, with 28½ votes going to Roosevelt and 65½ to Al Smith. This was a somewhat unpleasant surprise for the Roosevelt men and they got little consolation out of the second ballot, for on it Roosevelt made a gain of but a single vote. Their total gain of 11½ came mainly from Missouri, where the 12 Roosevelt votes of the first ballot increased to 18, with a corresponding loss to former Senator James A. Reed.

By this time it was clear that the Roosevelt assault had been hurled back, and the allies, who had been apparently trying all night to manufacture as many delays as possible, suddenly demanded action on their own account. This demand was sufficient to block an effort that the Roosevelt men made at 8.05 to adjourn until 4 P. M. It was opposed violently by New York, speaking through the clarion voice of Dudley Field Malone, and a standing vote showed such a formidable party against the adjournment that the proposal was withdrawn.

The second ballot probably took more time than any ever heard of before, even in a Democratic national convention The roll-call was begun at 5.17 A. M. and it was not until 8.05 that the result was announced. Thus the running time was nearly three hours. Two large States, Ohio and Pennsylvania, demanded to be polled, and there was a battle in the District of Columbia delegation that consumed a full hour. Two of the District delegates were Ritchie men, and they fought hard to throw off the unit rule and have their choice recorded, but Chairman Walsh decided that the rule bound them, and their votes were thus credited to Roosevelt. The same fate befell six Ritchie votes in the Michigan delegation on the third ballot.

Governor Ritchie polled 21 votes on the first ballot—Maryland's 16, 4 from Indiana and 1 from Pennsylvania. On the second ballot he gained $2\frac{1}{2}$ in Pennsylvania, making his total $23\frac{1}{2}$. Meanwhile Al Smith, who started off with $201\frac{3}{4}$, dropped to $194\frac{1}{4}$, and slight losses were also shown by Traylor, White, Byrd and Baker, and six of former Senator Reed's Missourians departed for the Roosevelt camp. Altogether the allies polled $487\frac{3}{4}$. On the first ballot, a few minutes before the roll-call began, Howard Bruce of Maryland estimated that they would poll 484 and that their irreducible minimum of shock troops, good for fifty ballots if necessary, was 425—40 more than would be needed to prevent Roosevelt from ever polling a two-thirds majority.

The all-night session was a horrible affair and by the time the light of dawn began to dim the spotlights, a great many delegates had gone back to their hotels or escaped to the neighboring speakeasies. When the balloting began shortly after 5 A. M., scores of them were missing and the fact explained the worst delays in the voting and especially some of the quarrels over the rights and dignities of alternates. When New York was called Jimmy Walker could not be found, but by the time the dreadful business of polling the immense State delegation, with its ninety regular members and eight members-at-large, neared an end, he somehow turned up and was presently saying something for the microphone and getting a round of applause for it.

The third ballot showed plainly that Roosevelt was not going to run the convention amuck, but the same evidence proved that the allies had likewise failed to knock him out. He was holding all of his principal delegations, and in addition he was making some small gains in the territory of the enemy. His total vote was 682 79-100, which showed an increase of five and a fraction over the second ballot and of sixteen over the first. This was surely not disaster. Nevertheless, it was still sufficient to fill the allies with hope and courage, for they had been in fear that the first Roosevelt rush would shake and break their lines, and that had certainly not happened.

The way the tide of battle was going was revealed dramatically by the attitude of the leaders on the two sides. All during the infernal night session the Roosevelt men had been trying to wear out and beat down the opposition, and to push on to a showdown. They opposed every motion to adjourn, and refused every other sort of truce. They wanted to get through with the speeches as soon as possible, but they were confident enough to be still willing to match speech with speech, and they did so until daylight. But after the first ballot they began to play for time, and after the second all of their early bellicosity had gone out of them.

The allies, meanwhile, were gaining in assurance. They knew that Al Smith was ready to talk of delivering his vote to one or another of them after the third ballot, and they were eager to reach it. But the Roosevelt men, by that stage, saw clearly that a hard fight was ahead, and so took their turn at playing for time. The combat of rhetoricians and rooters during the long, hot and weary hours of the night was depressingly typical of a Democratic national convention. The show was almost completely idiotic, with now and then a more or less rational speech to relieve it. Senator Tydings made one such speech, putting Governor Ritchie in nomination, and another was made by Richard F. Cleveland, son of Grover Cleveland, seconding him. A third came from William G. McAdoo in the interest of Garner. But the average was as low as one might look for at a ward club in a mean street and few of the delegates and fewer of the visitors seemed to pay any attention to what was said.

All sorts of grotesque female politicians, most of them with brassy voices and hard faces, popped up to talk to the radio audience back home. The evening session, in fact, had been postponed to nine o'clock to get a radio hookup and every fourth-rate local leader in the hall, male or female, tried for a crack at the microphone. More than once weary delegates objected that the Niagara of bilge was killing them and along toward four in the morning Josephus Daniels went to the platform and protested against it formally. But all of the nine candidates had to be put in nomination, and when they had been put in nomination all of them had to be seconded, not once, but two, four, six or a dozen times. Worse, their customers had to parade obscenely every time one of them was launched and some of the parades ran to nearly an hour.

Here one gang helped another. The Texans, who had a band, lent it to every other outfit that had a candidate, and it brayed and boomed for Ritchie, Byrd, Reed and Al Smith quite as cruelly as it performed for Garner. This politeness, of course, had to be repaid by its beneficiaries, and with interest. The Byrd band, clad in uniforms fit for Arctic exploration, did not let up for hours on end. And while it played one tune, the band of the Texans played another, and the official band in the gallery a third, and the elephantine pipe-organ a fourth. At one stage in the uproar a male chorus also appeared, but what it sang I can't tell you, nor which candidate it whooped and gargled for.

It was hard on the spectators in the galleries, but it was even harder on the delegates, for they had to march in a good many of the parades and they were hoofed and hustled when they kept their seats. Most of them, as is usual at a national convention, are beyond middle life, and a good many of them show obvious marks of oxidation.

Two have died since the convention began, a matter of only five days. Scores had to clear out of the hall during the night and seek relief in the corridors.

Toward three o'clock, a thunderstorm came up, and the extreme heat of the early evening began to lessen. By that time, a full half of the spectators had gone home, so the cops were able to open the great doors of the hall without running any risk of being rushed off their feet, and by dawn the place had become relatively comfortable. But then the sun began to shine down through the gallery windows, and presently the floor was a furnace again, and the delegates got out their foul handkerchiefs and resumed their weary mopping and panting.

Under such circumstances, there is always plenty of ill-humor. There is more of it than usual when Democrats meet, for they are divided into implacable factions, and each hates all the others. Many of the more wearisome maneuvers of the three roll calls were apparently suggested by mere malignancy. The Pennsylvanians, I was told, demanded to be polled simply to bring back to the hall some of their own delegates who had deserted the battlefield and gone home to bed. The row in the District of Columbia delegation was apparently two-thirds personal and only one-third political. And the Smith men carried on their relentless campaign of motions, protests and parliamentary inquiries mainly to annoy the Roosevelt men.

Toward the end the thing became a mere endurance match. It was plain after the second ballot that neither side was going to break, but the allies by now were hungry to punish the Roosevelt outfit, and they did so by opposing adjournment and by raising all sorts of nonsensical difficulties, some of which could be resolved only after long conferences on the platform and a copious consultation of precedent books and parliamentary lawyers.

Old Tom Walsh, the chairman, held out pretty well until eight o'clock, but then he began to cave in, and during the last hour the temporary chairman of the convention, the wet bridegroom, Senator Alben W. Barkley, of Kentucky, operated the bungstarter and struggled with the riddles that were thrown at him from the floor.

—XVIII—

THE PASSING OF
AL SMITH

[From the Baltimore Evening Sun, July 2, 1932]

Chicago, July 2

THE GREAT combat is ending this afternoon in the classical Democratic manner. That is to say, the victors are full of uneasiness and the vanquished are full of bile. It would be hard to find a delegate who believes seriously that Roosevelt can carry New York in November, or Massachusetts, or New Jersey, or even Illinois. All of the crucial wet States of the Northeast held out against him to the last ditch, and their representatives are damning him up hill and down dale today. Meanwhile, the Southern and Middle Western delegates are going home with a tattered Bible on one shoulder and a new and shiny beer seidel on the other, and what they will have to listen to from their pastors and the ladies of the W. C. T. U. is making their hearts miss every other beat.

The row ended quietly enough last night, but without the slightest sign of genuine enthusiasm. The galleries kept on howling for Al Smith to the finish, but Al himself sulked in his hotel, and placards in the lobbies this morning announced that most of his true friends would leave for Manhattan at noon. When, at 10.32 last night, Chairman Walsh announced the final vote, there was only the ghost of a cheer, and in less than a minute even the Roosevelt stalwarts were back in their seats and eager only for adjournment and a decent night's rest. The convention was worn out, but that was only part of the story. It was also torn by rancors that could not be put down. The Smith men all knew very well that the result was a good deal less a triumph for Roosevelt, who actually seemed to have few genuine friends in the house, than a defeat and rebuke for Smith. As for the Roosevelt men, they found themselves on their repeal honeymoon wondering dismally if the bride were really as lovely as she had seemed last Wednesday. Both sides had won and both had lost, but what each thought of was only the loss.

In all probability the Marylanders, though they lost their fight for Governor Ritchie, came out of the struggle with fewer wounds than any other delegation that played a part of any actual importance in the ceremonies. They had been beaten, but they had not made any enemies. They were on the bandwagon, but the Smith *bloc* had no cause to complain of them. They owed this comfortable result to the fine skill of Governor Ritchie himself. He was his own manager here, just as he had been his own manager in the preliminary campaign, and his coolness resisted a dozen temptations to run amuck and get into trouble. He took the whole thing calmly and good-naturedly, and showed not the slightest sign, at any stage, of the appalling buck fever which so often demoralizes candidates. He kept on good terms with the Smith outfit without getting any of its sulphurous smell upon him, and he submitted to the inevitable in the end in a dignified manner, and without any obscene embracing of Roosevelt. If Roosevelt is elected in November there is a swell place in the Cabinet waiting for him—that is, assuming that he wants it. And if Roosevelt is butchered by the implacable Smith men, then he will have another chance in 1936, and a far better one than he had this week, with the corpse of Al incommoding him.

As you all know by now, the final break to Roosevelt was brought on by Garner men from California. Garner's friends from Texas were prepared to stick to him until Hell froze over, but in California he was only a false face for McAdoo and Hearst, and McAdoo was far more bent upon punishing Smith for the events of 1924 than he was for nominating Texas Jack, just as Hearst was more eager to block his pet abomination, Newton D. Baker, than to name any other candidate. Hearst was quite willing on Thursday to turn to Ritchie, who was satisfactory to him on all the major issues, including especially the League of Nations. In fact, negotiations with him were in full blast Thursday afternoon, with Arthur Brisbane as the intermediary. But McAdoo had other ideas, chiefly relating to his own fortunes, and he pulled Hearst along. For one thing, McAdoo had a palpable itch for the Vice-Presidency. But above all he yearned to give Smith a beating, and he saw after the third ballot that Roosevelt would be the handiest stick for the job.

The actual nomination of Roosevelt after the turmoils of the all-night session went off very quietly. The delegates appeared in the hall all washed up, with clean collars, pressed suits and palpable auras of witch hazel and bay rum. The scavengers of the stadium had swept up the place, the weather had turned cool and there was the general letting down that always follows a hard battle. No one had had quite enough sleep, but everyone had had at least some. Chairman Walsh, who had been wilting visibly in the horrible early hours of the morning, was himself again by night, and carried on his operations with the bungstarter in his usual fair, firm and competent manner. He is a good presiding officer and he had got through the perils of the night session without disaster. Now he was prepared for the final scene and every spectator in the packed galleries knew where it would lead the plot and who would be its hero.

THE PASSING OF AL SMITH

California comes early on the roll, so there was no long suspense. McAdoo went up to the platform to deliver the State delegation in person. He must be close to seventy by now, if not beyond it, but he is still slim, erect and graceful, and as he made his little speech and let his eye rove toward the New York delegation he looked every inch the barnstorming Iago of the old school. Eight years ago at New York he led the hosts of the Invisible Empire against the Pope, the rum demon and all the other Beelzebubs of the Hookworm Belt, and came so close to getting the nomination that the memory of its loss must still shiver him. The man who blocked him was Al Smith, and now he was paying Al back.

If revenge is really sweet he was sucking a colossal sugar teat, but all the same there was a beery flavor about it that must have somewhat disquieted him. For he is a Georgia cracker by birth and has always followed his native pastors docilely, and it must have taken a lot of temptation to make him accept the ribald and saloonish platform. Here, indeed, revenge was working both ways, and if Al were a man of more humor he would have been smiling, too.

The other rebellious States fell into line without much ceremony, always excepting, of course, those which held out for Al to the end. Illinois was delivered by Mayor Cermak of Chicago, a Czech brought up on roast goose and Pilsner, and showing the virtues of that diet in his tremendous shoulders and sturdy legs. He spoke also for Indiana, which had been split badly on the first three ballots. When Maryland's turn came Governor Ritchie spoke for it from the floor, releasing its delegates and casting their votes for the winner, and a bit later on former Governor Byrd did the business for Virginia. In the same way Missouri was delivered by former Senator James A. Reed, who somewhat later came up to the platform and made a little speech, denouncing Samuel Insull and Lord Hoover in blistering terms and calling upon the Smith men to "fall in line like good soldiers and face the common enemy." Senator Reed spoke of the time as "this afternoon," though it was actually nearly ten o'clock at night. But no one noticed, for the all-night session had blown up all reckoning of time and space.

The whole proceedings, in fact, showed a

curiously fantastic quality. Here was a great party convention, after almost a week of cruel labor, nominating the weakest candidate before it. How many of the delegates were honestly for him I don't know, but certainly it could not have been more than a third. There was absolutely nothing in his record to make them eager for him. He was not only a man of relatively small experience and achievement in national affairs; he was also one whose competence was plainly in doubt, and whose good faith was far from clear. His only really valuable asset was his name, and even that was associated with the triumphs and glories of the common enemy. To add to the unpleasantness there was grave uneasiness about his physical capacity for the job they were trusting to him.

Yet here they were giving it to him, and among the parties to the business were a dozen who were patently his superior and of very much larger experience. For example, Tom Walsh, the chairman, one of the most diligent and useful Senators ever seen in Washington and a man whose integrity is unquestioned by anyone. For example, Carter Glass of Virginia, an irascible and almost fanatical fellow, but still a very able man and an immensely valuable public servant. For example, Reed of Missouri, the very picture and model of a Roman senator, whose departure from the Senate cost it most of its dramatic effectiveness and a good half of its power. Even McAdoo is certainly worth a dozen Franklin D. Roosevelts. As for Al Smith, though he is now going down hill fast, he was once worth a hundred. But the man who got the great prize was Roosevelt, and most of the others are now too old to hope for it hereafter.

The failure of the opposition was the failure of Al Smith. From the moment he arrived on the ground it was apparent that he had no plan, and was animated only by his fierce hatred of Roosevelt, the cuckoo who had seized his nest. That hatred may have had logic in it, but it was impotent to organize the allies and they were knocked off in detail by the extraordinarily astute Messrs. Farley and Mullen. The first two ballots gave them some hope, but it was lost on the third, for the tide by then was plainly going Roosevelt's way. Perhaps the Al of eight or ten years ago, or even of four years ago, might have achieved the miracle that the crisis called for, but it was far beyond the technique of the golf-playing Al of today. He has ceased to be the wonder and glory of the East Side and becomes simply a minor figure of Park avenue.

But in the midst of the débâcle he could at least steal some consolation from the fact that his foes were facing a very difficult and perhaps almost impossible campaign before the people. His sardonic legacy to his party is the platform, and especially the Prohibition plank. It will harass Roosevelt abominably until the vote is counted, and after that it may take first place among his permanent regrets. If his managers had had their way, there would have been a straddle comparable to the one made by the Republicans. But the allies rushed them so savagely that they were taken off their feet. That rush required little leadership. It was spontaneous and irresistible. The big cities poured out their shock troops for it.

The delegates went back to their hotels last night to the tune of "Onward, Christian Soldiers." It was the first time that the tune had been heard in the convention, and probably the first time it had been heard in the hall. But playing it was only a kind of whistling in the dark. For five days the bands had been laboring far different hymns, and their echoes still sounded along the rafters.

—XIX—

WHERE ARE WE AT?[1]

[From the Baltimore Evening Sun, July 5, 1932]

THERE IS no disguising the fact that beating Lord Hoover and the Injun with Roosevelt Minor and the Texas Bearcat is not going to be easy. The betting odds tell the story quite as well as long argument. At the time when the allies seem to be prevailing, the Chicago sports offered 5 to 1 that Governor Ritchie, if nominated, would defeat Hoover. But when the nomination went to Roosevelt they began offering 5 to 1 that Hoover would win. Bookmakers, of course, sometimes err, just as the other varieties of

[1] This was printed on the editorial page of the *Evening Sun*.

mathematicians err. But in this case their guess is also the guess of the majority of practical politicians.

Mr. Roosevelt enters the campaign with a burden on each shoulder, and neither is a light one. The first is the burden of his own limitations. He is one of the most charming of men, but like many another very charming man he leaves on the beholder the impression that he is also somewhat shallow and futile. It is hard to say precisely how that impression is produced: maybe his Christian Science smile is to blame, or the tenor overtones in his voice. Whatever the cause, the fact is patent that he fails somehow to measure up to the common concept of a first-rate man. Moreover, there is his physical disability. He struggles against it in a most gallant manner, and will certainly never let it down him, but all the same it would be idle to say that he is as fit as a normal man.

The burden on his other shoulder is even heavier. It is the burden of party disharmony. As I have so often noted in this place, the Democrats are really divided into two parties, and each distrusts and dislikes the other more than it distrusts and dislikes the common enemy. No man can become the Democratic standard-bearer without leading one faction against the other, and then having to face the losing faction's lust for revenge. At Houston, four years ago, the beaten Bible students from the South and Middle West walked out on Al Smith, holding their noses. And at Chicago last week the beaten Al Smith men from the big cities walked out on Roosevelt, to the sinister tune of Bronx cheers.

There were, of course, plenty of sincere Roosevelt men in the convention, but they fell far short of the strength needed to make the nomination. It would probably be safe to say that they numbered no more than 200 altogether. The rest of the necessary votes came from delegates who were not primarily Roosevelt men at all, but simply anti-Smith men. Some of them were Ku Kluxers who revolted against Al in 1928, and were eager only to smash him again. Others were more seemly fellows who believed honestly that he had caused enough trouble for the party, and ought to retire. Together, these factions probably mustered 400 votes, divided God knows how. The 200 really sincere Roose-

velt votes, added to them, made 600, leaving
the nomination still in the air. It was achieved by
the flop of the slippery McAdoo, who hated
Smith even more than the frank Ku Kluxers hated
him, and was full of a yen to ruin him.

That this ruin was accomplished I verily believe. It was due in part to the strength and fe-
rocity of the factions thus lined up against poor
Al, but even more to his own folly and inapti-
tude. From the moment he arrived in Chicago
he made only blunders. First, he insisted idiotically that he could get the nomination himself,
and announced that he would fight for it to the
last ditch. Then, when it became plain that he
could halt Roosevelt only by stepping down and
organizing and leading the Allies, he approached
the job so clumsily that they quickly deserted
him and turned to former Senator James A.
Reed. And finally, after letting it be known that
if the worst came to the worst he would take to
the platform and destroy Roosevelt utterly with
a brutal and unanswerable speech, he fled from
the hall in silence, his tail between his legs.

What has happened to Al I do not know. But
that he is no longer the resilient and indomitable

leader of yesteryear must be plain to everyone. The Happy Warrior has been transformed by some black magic into an ill-humored and ineffective fellow, bent only upon a melodramatic vengeance. He may get it in November, but if so it will do him no good. For he is almost as dead, politically speaking, as John W. Davis or James M. Cox. When he walked out of the convention nearly 200 delegates were still faithful to him, but no such number will ever vote for him again.

If, however, his defeat disposes of him, it does not rid the party of his ghost. That ghost will walk on election day, and its operations, I suspect, will be painfully visible in the old Smith territory, which is to say, in the big cities of the East and Middle West. Roosevelt will probably carry all the Southern States that Al lost in 1928, despite the difficulties that the repeal plank is bound to raise in some of them, but he will certainly lose New York, and there is little chance that he will carry Massachusetts and its tributaries. He may win nevertheless, but if he does it will be by a kind of miracle.

Almost any of the other candidates before the

convention (I except, of course, Al) would have stood a better chance, if nominated, of beating Hoover. This is especially true of Governor Ritchie. He showed a very high degree of political skill while the Smith-Roosevelt combat was on, and though he failed to get on the ticket in the end he at least came out with many new friends and greatly enhanced prestige. Hundreds of delegates went home regretting that he had not been nominated. He would have been strong precisely where Roosevelt is weak—in the big cities of the Northeast—and it would have been easy for him to conquer the South.

But Roosevelt won, and now the party begins the campaign with a candidate who has multitudes of powerful and implacable enemies, and is in general far too feeble and wishy-washy a fellow to make a really effective fight. Soon or late the voters of the country are bound to ask themselves two questions. The first is: In what way precisely is he better than Hoover? And the second is, What has he ever done to justify making him President? These questions are going to be hard to answer. Ritchie might have answered them, but not Roosevelt. He got the nomination without adequate reason, and that lack of reason will haunt the campaign.

The downfall of Smith brought back a whole flock of political cadavers, some of them resident in the boneyard for four, eight and even twelve years. If it was astonishing to see William G. McAdoo return to the fray, it was even more astonishing to see Josephus Daniels and A. Mitchell Palmer. I confess that I almost fainted myself when I discovered that Palmer, as Roosevelt's agent, was writing the platform. He got a dreadful beating on his Prohibition plank, which was rejected ignominiously by the really wet wets, but he played an important part in the proceedings otherwise, and if Roosevelt is elected he will no doubt return to Washington, and resume his patriotic assault upon the Bill of Rights.

It is a good measure of Roosevelt that Palmer is his friend and supporter. Try to imagine an honest Progressive resorting to such company! I often wondered, during the grotesque agonies of the convention, what the Hon. Thomas J. Walsh thought of it, but I was too discreet to ask him. It was Walsh, in the closing days of the Wilson administration, who put an end to the

Palmer reign of terror, and yet here the two of them were lying down in the same bed! But that, alas, is always the fate of Democrats. Either they must lie with their natural enemies, or must go without sleep at all.

My guess is that Roosevelt, before the campaign proceeds very far, will try to pull some of the teeth of the repeal plank. He essayed a preliminary yank in his speech of acceptance, by denouncing the saloon. The really wet wets are not against the saloon: they are in favor of it, and they hope to see it restored—if not under its old name, then under another. But the biblical scholars from the South and Middle West will have to do a great deal of yowling against it to placate their pastors and the ladies of the W. C. T. U., and they will demand some aid and comfort from the standard-bearer. Everyone will recall how long he kept silent about Prohibition when repeal first became a serious issue. But this time silence will not be enough: he will have to say something. If what he says is uncompromisingly wet, he will be in trouble in the Hookworm Belt, and if what he says shows the slightest dryness his ruin will be complete in the Babylons.

Altogether, the right hon. gentleman is on a hot spot. I shall vote for him as in duty bound. Anything to get rid of Hoover and his camorra of Republican blacklegs! I'd vote for a Chinaman to beat them, or even a Methodist bishop. But I greatly fear that there will be insufficient Americans of like mind to reëstablish and perpetuate the Roosevelt dynasty.

—XX—

THE END OF PROHIBITION[1]

[From the Baltimore Evening Sun, July 11, 1932]

THE VICTORY of the wets at the Democratic National Convention was so colossal that it left the victors almost as upset as the vanquished. They were like an army that had made an attack, found the enemy's trenches deserted, and then gone galloping for miles into his country. All of the wet leaders on the ground were so astonished that they were almost speechless. What they had looked for was the adoption of the original majority plank, prepared by the talented A. Mitchell Palmer under the personal eye of Governor Roosevelt. But what they got was the forthright, uncompromising, whole-hog plank of the drip-

[1] This was printed on the editorial page of the *Evening Sun*.

ping wet faction led by Senator David I. Walsh of Massachusetts and Major E. Brooke Lee of Maryland—a minority that somehow transformed itself, between noon of June 29 and 3 P. M., into an overwhelming and irresistible majority.

How such things happen is always mysterious. Long rows of books have been written on the psychological processes underlying them, but they still remain essentially unfathomable. All that may be said of a surety is that men in mobs sometimes change their minds with an alarming suddenness. The delegates to a national convention constitute a kind of mob, and two times out of three they act as one—suddenly, unexpectedly and irrationally. The fact that one can never predict what they are going to do is what wears out the newspaper reporters told off to report their so-called deliberations. It is impossible to see ahead of them, and even difficult to follow them.

During their late convention the Democrats gave two instructive exhibitions of this tendency to run amuck. First they arose without warning and tore Prohibition limb from limb, and then, after stopping Roosevelt and opening the way for a long and juicy combat, they leaped into his arms with horrible hosannahs. The first phenomenon was really more remarkable than the second. They might have stopped far short of their 200-proof plank and still gone much further than the pussyfooting Republicans. But for some reason or other they decided to finish the job at one stupendous crack, and when the fog of battle cleared away there was nothing left of the Prohibitionists save a few ears, a blood-stained copy of the Methodist Book of Discipline, and a disorderly heap of empty collection plates.

There is still some mopping up to do, and it will probably be a year more before the schooners really begin to slide over the bars, but I believe that it is quite safe to say that Prohibition died on June 29, 1932, aged twelve years, five months and thirteen days. If you doubt the fact, just regard the present state of mind of the Prohibitionists. One faction, made up of most of the professionals, is sulking in silence, trying to make up its mind what to do. Another was lately meeting at Indianapolis, trying to revive the old Prohibition party of thirty years ago, and finding it impossible to find presentable standard-bearers. But the third and largest faction has simply thrown up the sponge.

The sponge, in fact, was in the air before the Democratic assassins got to Chicago, and even before the Republicans got there. Lord Hoover, greatly underestimating, like the rest of us, the extent and horse-power of the wet uprising, was perfectly willing to trade with Bishop Cannon and company again, just as he had traded with them in 1928. The last word heard from him, in fact, had been a ringing denunciation of repeal. But when his jackals got to Chicago, and began to talk to the first comers among the delegates, they saw at once that there would have to be a compromise with the wets, and when it was effected at last, after a great deal of frantic telephoning to Washington, the wets had their beer-keg and the drys had only the bunghole.

The drys, at the time, professed to be satisfied, and that profession was given some color of plausibility by the fact that the wet extremists, led by Dr. Nicholas Murray Butler, were beaten in committee and on the floor. But the more closely the Republican straddle was examined, the more plain it became that there was little consolation in it for honest Prohibitionists. It simply threw Prohibition overboard—with a rope attached to it, to be sure, but that rope was around its neck. Not a single dry, given his free choice, would have approved the plank, nor any single sliver of it. It was, from the dry standpoint, an abject surrender to the enemy.

The Democratic plank, of course, was even worse—in fact, much worse—and therein lies one of the remaining hopes of the dry professionals. They believe, first, that Lord Hoover, before the campaign has gone very far, will throw them some sort of bone—that there is still enough decency in him to make him give his old allies a hand in their trouble. They believe, second, that Roosevelt is the weakest candidate the Democrats could have named, and that his chances of winning in November are very bad. And they believe, third, that if he is defeated they will be able to make it appear that his defeat was a rebuke to the wets, and that the dry cause will thus take on new life.

There are some significant ifs here, but all the same the reasoning is sound enough. It is characteristic of Democratic imbecility that the party convention, after making victory a 1-to-5 shot by adopting an uncompromisingly wet platform, immediately converted it into a 5-to-1 shot by nominating a feeble and dubious candidate. With Ritchie it would have been a walkover, but with Roosevelt it is only a hope. And that hope is certainly not given any material support by the fact that the nomination was effected by the slippery politics of a gang of very recently converted drys, and to the rage and disgust of some of the oldest and most heroic wet veterans in the hall.

Thus both factions left Chicago sore—the ex-drys because the platform went too far for them, and was very likely to get them into serious trouble at home, and the *Ur*-wets because they had failed to put a standard-bearer of their own choice upon it. Eminent men now make gallant efforts to assuage these wounds, but their success is certainly not assured. The boys from the Bible country are being boiled in oil at this very minute. Their pastors tackle them from the front, and the beldames of the W. C. T. U. from the rear. It remains to be seen how much they will have to compromise, and to what extent they will pull their punches in November. And it remains to be seen whether Mr. Roosevelt, with McAdoo and company on his neck, can really win back the Smith following in the big cities of the Northeast.

But even if Roosevelt loses, Prohibition will still be dead. All the imponderables now run against it. The legend of its invincibility has blown up. The big cities were against it from the start, but until six months ago it seemed to be invulnerable in the smaller towns and villages. But now even the hicks have turned upon it, and begin to demand raucously that it be shoveled away. At the Democratic convention only two States voted solidly for the milder of the rival planks, and in the delegation of each there were plenty of earnest and even rabid wets. When I saw Iowa, South Carolina and North Dakota cast their votes unanimously for the wet-wet plank, I knew that I was in attendance at a death-bed, and when I saw even Kansas come within four votes of doing likewise, I heard a gurgle that could have but one meaning.

What remains, as I have said, is the mopping

up. It will not be as facile as some of the more romantic wets seem to think, for the professional Prohibitionists are tough babies, and will give the mortician more than one stiff wallop before he gets them underground. It is even likely that some small successes are still ahead of them. They know how to play one party against the other, and have already done it very successfully in the Senate, where, as I write, the beer bill is halted by mutual suspicions. They will take a deep breath if Roosevelt loses to Lord Hoover, and do some loud hollering. But all the same they are licked, and the wiser heads among them are well aware of it. If they really run a ticket of their own, they will return straightway to their old rôle of harmless cranks.

My hopes, at the moment, run in two directions. First, I hope that no decent wet will be deceived by the political scoundrels who are now deserting the drys by the regiment and army corps. They were street-walkers when they took orders from the Anti-Saloon League, and they remain street-walkers today. Let them be retired to private life as soon as possible. Second, I hope that no one, especially here in Maryland, will forget the tremendous public services of Capt. William H. Stayton, founder of the Association Against the Prohibition Amendment. The victory owes more to his indomitability than to anything else. He was in the forefront of the fray, battling heroically, when many of those who are now applauded were far in the rear, disheartened and impotent. If any Baltimorean in a hundred years has deserved a monument, he is that man.

GOD SAVE THE REPUBLIC!

A NOTE
ON THE TYPE
IN WHICH THIS BOOK IS SET

This book is composed on the linotype in Bodoni, so called after its designer, Giambattista Bodoni (1740–1813), a celebrated Italian scholar and printer. Bodoni planned his type especially for use on the more smoothly finished papers that came into vogue late in the eighteenth century. Characteristics that will be noted are the square serifs without fillet and the marked contrast between the light and heavy strokes.

SET UP, PRINTED, AND BOUND BY
HARRIS WOLFF ESTATE
NEW YORK
PAPER MADE BY
S. D. WARREN CO.
BOSTON, MASS.